EVERYWHERE MEANS SOMETHING TO SOMEONE

The people's guidebook to Dover

Commissioned by Dover Town Council

Strange Cargo

The Factory · 43 Geraldine Road
Cheriton, Folkestone, Kent, UK CT19 4BD

www.strangecargo.org.uk
info@strangecargo.org.uk

Strange Cargo is a Registered Charity, No.1068396

Design by Scarlett Rickard
Cover image by Loz Chalk

ISBN: 9-781738-518005

If you were to ask, say, a New Yorker, a Parisian or a Berliner about Folkestone, or Margate, it is probable that they would have heard of neither. If, on the other hand, you mentioned Dover it is highly likely there would be instant recognition.

'The White Cliffs of Dover' — said someone cleverer than me — are to the UK what the Hollywood sign is to California. Their whiteness gives rise to the British soubriquet 'Albion', *albus* being Latin for chalk. Instantly recognisable and immortalised in wartime song, the White Cliffs are the gleaming teeth of England, historically gnashing across the Channel at continental Europe, rebuffing the French, Spanish and the Luftwaffe, while also smiling, welcoming millions of European visitors and international overland trade.

Despite this recognition, Dover has something of a dilemma. Very little of the traffic coming through the port actually stays in Dover. Freight heads directly to London or further north, while the vast majority of tourist traffic disperses across Kent and elsewhere.

To a degree they can be forgiven. Arriving from France and driving off the ferry, the visitor will be aware of the majesty of the cliffs receding behind them, giving way to the fading elegance of a run of Regency villas and hotels. However, with an eye on the road, within seconds you are through the traffic lights, and up the hill on the A20 and away, out of Dover altogether.

I have an urge to shout out to everyone to TURN LEFT or TURN RIGHT, as within that half a mile drive are hidden many of Dover's unique Heritage assets: a Saxon Church ruin, a Roman painted villa, an Arts and Crafts customs house, several fortresses camouflaged in the Western Heights, accessed by a hidden set of monumental spiral stairs. There is a disused station from the golden age of travel frozen in time, out at sea... and you drive over the spot where a Bronze Age boat was discovered, 3,500 years old — a sign that Dover was up and running and trading when Tutankhamen was still on the throne.

Within the town itself, there are more gems, hiding in plain sight. If you step out of Wetherspoon's (once The Grand Metropole Hotel, its monogrammed initials still visible to the balcony ironwork) into the pedestrianised Cannon Street, right opposite you is the doorway of St Mary's Church, built on a Roman site. Its carved Norman doorway, dating back to 1086, is still in use. At the other end of the street hides the tiny St Edmund's Chapel (1252 AD), a hardy survivor of the Reformation; while just round the corner the medieval Town Hall — the Maison Dieu — is currently under restoration, revealing the William Burgess Arts and Crafts Gothic revival interiors. Just behind runs the chalk stream of the River Dour, where wild brown trout often find their way into the centre of town.

My approach is most often from the opposite viewpoint, coming down the A20 from the London direction. I always catch my breath as the vista of Dover Harbour opens up in front of me — a vast basin with shipping of all sizes bobbing about like toys in a bath, a world-class fairytale castle perched above on high. Below is the Dover I'd like you to see: the gateway to England, proud and enduring and hiding its light under a bushel.

Hopefully, this book will reveal some of its secrets.

Welcome to Dover.

Peter Cocks

INTRODUCTION

This is not a regular guidebook, but a compilation of many hundreds of stories from local people about where they live. The aim is to encourage anyone exploring Dover to view the town from the perspective of the people who know it well.

At Strange Cargo we always involve other people in our work, so their contribution is visible in the end result. The title of the book gives a glimpse into what we set out to do, which was to discover anything and everything about places in Dover that have significance to someone. Whether a location, building, object, or a memory of an experience, people have recalled traces of their own — or other people's — lives lived in the town. Even the most ordinary or unexpected location can hold significance, because of what has happened there; this knowledge is mostly the preserve of local people.

We don't have a set of rules about what to share, we simply let the guidebook find its own form through what people decide is important to them about the place. We frequently suggest, when prompted, for people to "tell us what you'd tell a good friend visiting for the first time." Some locations appear more than once, which reflects their significance. Once gifted, those bits of knowledge are overlaid across Dover's terrain to paint an intimate picture.

Someone suggested we stand out on the end of pier and look back at the town, because from this vantage point we would be able to see two Dovers. We didn't quite understand what they meant, but after spending more than a year viewing Dover through the eyes of local people, this comment made sense.

The first Dover that comes into focus is the place where people live: 21st century Dover, with its day-to-day joys and challenges; a strategically positioned port town, whose inhabitants mostly live their lives on the valley slopes overlooking the river Dour. There are many generations of local families whose knowledge stretches back, who can recall different times; and there are newer residents whose varied lives have more recently led them to call Dover their home.

The second Dover took longer to come into focus: alongside Dover's modern, 24-hour comings and goings is this mysterious, hidden place which only local people really know about. Within its boundaries are overgrown paths to underground forts, ruined Saxon churches, miles of half-forgotten chalk tunnels, mythical stone cairns, sunken treasure and sunken ships and stories of pilgrims, knights, pirates, and battles fought by sea and air. It is a place arrived at by millions of people, but seldom visited. Dover is a sleeping giant that has a sense that it is starting to stir.

Change is a constant process and it should be embraced, but the places we all occupy connect us to each other, and knowing what they mean to other people is something to be valued, providing the foundation for everything that comes next.

Everywhere Means Something to Someone – The People's Guidebook to Dover has been commissioned by Town Clerk Allison Burton, Dover Town Council.

Brigitte Orasinski – Artistic Director, Strange Cargo

PEOPLE WHO HAVE CONTRIBUTED STORIES FOR THIS GUIDEBOOK

Aarron Monaco
Adeline Reidy
Alan Goldup
Alex Davies
Alfred Phillips
Allison Burton
Amy West
Andrew Ashton
Andrew Baldwin
Andrew Greenwood
Andy Milton
Angela Godfrey
Angela Wakefield
Anne Wimsett
Annette Marsh
Annie Kinnear
Barbara Hatton
Barry O'Brien
Bettina Southey
Bob Chicalors
Bradley (The Forge
   youth club)

Brandon Mupfurutsa
Brenda Drew
Brian Constable
Brigitte Orasinski
Cameron Lee
Cameron Simcock
Carol Duffield
Carol Mercer
Caroline Gibson
Carrick Richards
Cathy Forbes
Charles Holland
Charley Vines
Charlotte Fielding
Charmaine Simmons
Christopher Seaden
Christopher Smith
Corinne Bentley
Corinne D'Cruz
Dan Biddle
Darren Blyth
Dave Rimmell

Dave Robinson
David Bruce
David De Min
David Phillips
David Todd
Debby Ransley
Deborah Gasking
Denise Smith
Diederik Smet
Donna Rea
Dot Blackman
Dover Greeters
Ed Platt
Elizabeth Dimech
Emma Brimson
Emma Panda
Emma Taylor
Emma-Dawn Wood
Ewan Gartshore
Faith (The Forge
   youth club)
Fiona Hobbs

Frances Campbell
Frazer Doyle
Gareth Garside
George Cory
Gerald Doolin
Gillian Barlow
Gilly Lucas
Graham Fernee
Greg Taylor
Hannah Prizeman
Harold Red
Harry Reid
Hayley Balch
Hector Bowles
Jake Michael
Jake Wellard
James Calver
Jamie Maddocks
Jane Allcock
Jane Frances
Janet Pott
Jean Marsh

Jeanneke Hodges
Jennifer Carding
Jenny Olpin
Jeremy Cope
Jim Gleason
Jim Green
Jo Boughtwood
Joanna Jones
John Bird
John Robinson
Jon Iveson
Josh Leppenwell
Joshua Dowle
Kai (The Forge
   youth club)
Karen Byrne
Karen Dry
Karen Walkden
Katherine Webb
Kayla (The Forge
   youth club)
Keith Barraclough

Kim De Min
Kim Keeler
Lesley Stephenson
Lincoln (The Forge
   youth club)
Linda Davies
Lindsay Powell
   Williams
Lisa Oulton
Lisbeth Tull
Liz Demich
Liz Hayes
Liz Smith
Louella Ward
Loz Chalk
Lucia Power
Madelaine McNeill
Mandy Whall
Margaret Stanley
Maria Barrett
Marie Kelly-Thomas
Mark Hodgson
Mark Rodman
Martha Smith

Martin Crowther
Martin Smith
Martin Turner
Martyn Webster
Mary Glow
Mary Huntley
Mary Smye-Rumsby
Matt Rowe
Matt Wilson
Matthew
Matthews Crow
Mel Durrant
Melanie Chalk
Melanie Jacobs
Melanie Wrigley
Michael Banks
Michael Dowling
Mike McFarnell
Mike Stampton
Mike Vanderhoeven
Neil Rix
Nicholas Cobb
Nicholas Ward
Nick Varian

Nigel Collor
Olivia Franklin
Pam Tonothy
Pat Williams
Patricia Knight
Patrick Smith
Patti Pike
Paul Reeder
Paul Smye-Rumsby
Paul Wrigley
Paula Brown
Paula Williams
Peter Cocks
Petra Crow
Poppy Bell-Wallace
Quaid Ricketts
Rebecca Sawbridge
Rebecca Sperini
Richard Speller
Richie Moment
Robert Bennett
Roy Hatton
Ruby Cooke
Ruby-Mai Mackintosh

Ruth Griffiths
Sam Marlow
Samara Scott
Sandra Malho
Sarah Sharp
Scarlett Rickard
Shane Smith
Shiela Cope
Simon Bill
Simon Everett
Sophie Jessup
Stephen Benn
Stephen Moseling
Steve Barrett
Steve Chance
Steve Cross
Steve Popple
Steve Timms
Sunrise Café Team
Susan Howell
Susan Jones,
   Right Worshipful
   Town Mayor of
   Dover & Speaker

of the
Confederation
of Cinque Ports
Susan Pilcher
Tammy West
Teresa Jennings
Terrie Willsher
Terry Sutton
Theresa Smith
Timothy Smithen
Toby Oakes
Tony Poole
Tony Simcock
Tracey Hubbard
Trish Kansy
Valerie Bale
Valerie Bawes
Valerie Bowes
Valerie Drew
Vronni Ward
Wendy Grieve
Wendy Hadden
Wendy Wilkins
Young Skaters

EVERYWHERE MEANS SOMETHING TO SOMEONE

Between the pages of this guidebook you will find practical suggestions for places to visit, to eat, locations to explore, and knowledge shared by people who know those special places to walk, ponder and relax. You will read about family life within local people's living memory, alongside histories that stretch much further back in time. There are recent accounts of Pride parades and lantern parades through the town centre, sitting alongside recollections of long-ago royal visits and ancient ceremonies. Some cherished, but long-gone establishments don't have a page of their own, but are fondly remembered, such as the Churchill Snooker Hall that for twenty years occupied the old Townsend Club building on London Road; run by Pete Dry and Mick Graham; its Winston Churchill clock is still visible to passers-by. A menagerie of creatures makes an appearance — a tiger, monkeys, polar bear, foxes, and all manner of birds. And have you ever wondered about the hump in the road along York Street? This is the only visible indication of the ancient fortress buried deep under the road. We've been told that behind Snargate Street there are still grapevines and fig trees on land that was once cultivated by the Romans.

We cannot offer a guarantee that everything you read is a fact; but then that is not the point of this guidebook. What is most important is that these are home truths, the common currency of Dover people, and what they share with each other. We hope you enjoy finding out more about Dover and we'd like to offer our sincere thanks to all the people that have made this guidebook possible. Some places just beyond the town's boundaries are included as their stories are too interesting not to share.

EVERYWHERE MEANS SOMETHING TO SOMEONE

Strange Cargo is a participatory arts company based on the Kent coast. Everything we do involves a broad invitation to local people to get involved and to help contribute to shaping the outcome of the work. In the 30 years we have been in existence this approach has engaged many thousands of people in creating carnivals, light festivals, exhibitions, award-winning public artworks and many books. The most important part of our work is to ensure local residents are visible, involved and contribute to shaping the cultural offer of where they live.

Our special place in Dover is Coombe Hole (or, on some maps, Hole Coombe). Tucked away behind Connaught Park and St Mary's Cemetery, it's only a few minutes' walk away from our house, yet somehow we had never discovered it until the 2020 lockdown. Venturing out on one of our evening walks to the buttercup-covered field above Astley Avenue — another of our lockdown discoveries — we looked across the valley to the natural bowl and decided to head there on our next walk.

We were delighted to discover views over the town towards the sea in one direction, and across the bowl towards the cemetery in the other. Our boys loved the many different paths they could take down into the bowl and up again, meeting us at the other side. Best of all was when snow arrived in February 2021, during the second spell of school closures — we knew just where to head with our sledge (that had been waiting in the shed for snow for many years)! Careering down the slopes on our family sledging trip was exhilarating for all of us, and a memory to be treasured.

Photograph: Rebecca Sperini

My aunt told me a story from her days as a schoolgirl living in the town during the First World War. When the wind blew from the east you could sometimes hear the distant rumble of gunfire from the Western Front. Later, she used a piece of shrapnel from World War Two as a doorstop.

16th October, 1987. I had full scaffold up around a part of this building and, at one o'clock in the morning when it started to get really windy, I was a bit concerned so I came down here to check it. And lucky enough I never lost no boards or nothing off the scaffold, but I witnessed a little Fiat car being blown up the seafront — it rolled all the way, right across the front of these buildings here and right to the end of Harbour House there. The other side of the road, there on the corner, there used to be toilets, and it got blown through the fence and that's where it stayed.

On the other side, the roofs all got blown off — and I never lost a single board, absolutely amazing. There were lampposts being blown over and snapped off, it was very shocking. I was out very early in the morning, and I had another big scaffold out at River and I went round to check that. As I drove past Crabble Corn Mill a row of trees came down behind me like bang, bang, bang, bang, like great big pine trees, 60, 70 foot high.

Photograph: Mary Glow

EVERYWHERE MEANS SOMETHING TO SOMEONE

While much of Dover's heritage is obvious, like the Castle, perhaps Dover's rarest asset is hidden away up several flights of stairs in a darkened room, behind glass doors that open on to an Indiana Jones-level discovery.

Unearthed in 1992 during roadworks on the A20, the remains of a Bronze Age boat were found approximately where the pedestrian underpass now runs. Now preserved in its own gallery, it is an electrifying touchstone to our ancient past.

Apparently silted up in a small inlet to the river Dour, the boat was constructed about 3,500 years ago from oak planks stitched together with yew lashings, and caulked with moss and animal fat. On a timeline, that puts it around 1500 years before Jesus Christ, around the end of Tutankhamen's dynasty and with ancient Greece in full swing... which makes it the world's oldest seagoing vessel.

While it cannot be proven, there is plenty of forensic evidence to suggest that such boats crossed the Channel, exchanging glass, pottery and bronze with our European neighbours and, while trading between here and France has never been without its frictions, this demonstrates that there has always been a way.

Photograph: Rebecca Sperini

There used to be ship just off the entrance there, sort of in line with that lighthouse. There's a new bit of pier there that wasn't there then, it wasn't built that long ago. Years ago, during the war, they sunk a few ships in the harbour to stop submarines and stuff coming through, and that was one of the ships that had been sunk in the entrance.

On a neap tide you used to see part of the mast, a piece of metal that was on the funnel sticking out the water. But it used to restrict the cruise ships coming in and out, so they got a big barge with a big, long arm on it and they cut the ship up and they pulled it all out of the water. It's just the one they took out — I don't know actually how many were dropped down there during the war, like.

Photograph: Mary Glow

There's nowhere else in the world that has two Roman lighthouses, or Pharos. There are only four places in the world that have still got their Roman Pharos. If you know anyone that knows about any others, I would love to know.

....

Today the Pharos is only a four-storey building at 19 metres, with the top floor section being a medieval restoration. Originally it had six levels at 20 metres — it could have even been eight levels high according to some Roman historians.

According to the *Journal of Antiquities,* a beacon would have burned every night on the top of the lighthouse enabling Roman sailing vessels crossing the Channel between Gaul and Britannia to navigate their way into the harbour without encountering the rocky headland. The lighthouse would have been manned all through the night by a watch of sailors from the Classis Britannica naval fleet — galley crews, who may have camped beside the harbour and, with the help of slaves, built the Pharos as a replica of the design of Emperor Caligula's.

....

Each time a new Lord Warden of the Cinque Ports is sworn in, it is done on the remains of the second Roman Pharos at Drop Redoubt.

Photograph: Amy West

My nan moved to Dover from India — her parents were there in the army. They came back and lived here. She was a photographer, and she worked at a shop in Dover. She was maybe, like, 18 and she did some time as a photographer in the RAF in the 1950s. Then she met my grandad and stopped working.

Their lifestyle was so country, and they used to have a smallholding. We had it in our family for 30 years; we used to go up there and take care of the chickens, ducks, goats and geese. It was hard, as you can't just go and get a lawn mower, but they had a goat to keep the plants down. Goats are good little lawn mowers.

We used to joke and call my grandad's shed holy ground because it was built with bricks and materials from a church that was bombed. They used to pretend it was holy. It's gone now. It's mad that it was in my family for so long. It was in Astley Avenue. On one side there's allotments and, if you keep going up that road, that's where it was, near Rix Scaffolding.

Photograph: Susan Pilcher

Past where the main road curves round into the Eastern Docks, inside the cliff there are massive tanks built into the pier. They're oil tanks, and there used to be pipes which are still there which run out under the water, from the Eastern Arm all the way round to the entrance to the lighthouse at the western entrance. The idea was that if the German fleet ever came in, someone would turn the oil on, flood the harbour with it and set it on fire. It's all still built into the pier, but nobody would know.

Photograph: Rebecca Sperini

Aycliffe Estate was brand new when we moved in. It was a lovely house, with running water! I was six and I had a younger brother, and it was a neighbourhood full of families. We had a nice garden. On one side was the hill that led over to Maxton, and the other side was Shakespeare Beach. There used to be steps going down to the beach, but they had to be renewed due to subsidence. At the bottom of the road was the Co-Op and a shop called Taskers. We were given 1d (one old penny) and would buy penny chews. People were relocated there from all over. I go to the Women's Institute with my friend Marcia, who I went to school with, in the old school out at Aycliffe. I used to work at Court's, the furniture shop; it's now Hine's the jewellers.

Photograph: Mary Glow

EVERYWHERE MEANS SOMETHING TO SOMEONE

The Maison Dieu was a medieval hospital founded in the 13th century by Hubert de Burgh, which was passed to Henry III in 1257. It was a hospital right through to the Reformation, when it became a victualling yard: a public place for supplying the Royal Navy with bread, wine, beer and meat, fish... you name it. It was bought by the Corporation to turn it into a town hall, law courts and gaol in the 1830s.

The old gaol was on the site of the current Dover Museum. When the Corporation outgrew it, they bought the Maison Dieu hospital off the military and built a new museum, with Market Hall below and the Museum above, in 1848. They moved the Corporation's legal stuff up to the new Town Hall, which has been repurposed many times. Maison Dieu was designed by neo-gothic designer of note William Burgess in 1893, and was built on the remains of a 1290 hall. The chapel, built in the 1220s, is inside and was re-decked as a court hall with a floor inserted. The 1290s hall is still in there, but just with an extra deck in it. It's a fascinating building. The building will reopen summer 2025.

Photograph: Strange Cargo

The horse trough is an itinerant object. It's now just behind the St Mary's Church, but it used to be in the Market Square, and before that it was by the tram shelter in Charlton. Before that, it was at Commercial Quay. An interesting thing, which doesn't have a label on it, but it was put where it is now as it always seemed to be in the way.

Photograph: Mary Glow

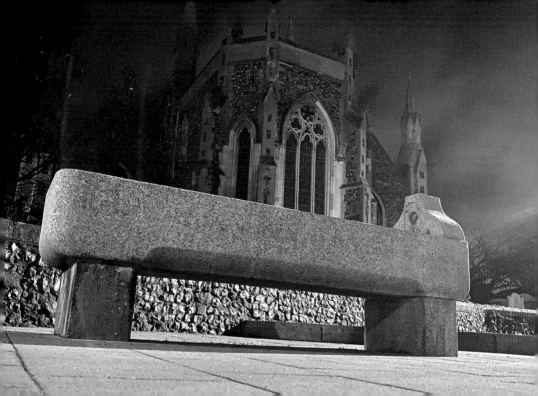

The Dover Town Council offices were built as the Victualling Officer's quarters in 1665, and eventually became Dover Library, after all sorts of other things, including being the private home for one of the pioneers of mountaineering.

....

There are tunnels under Dover Town Council's offices, five of them which go off in different directions under this building. We don't know where they all used to go because the Victorians plonked the sewers through them and chopped them all off, so they now stretch about 20 feet, but I'm absolutely positive one went to the Maison Dieu, because this was the Victualling House. We think one went to the College, and there's another that clearly went to the Castle. There is a ghost story here. We never really talk about smuggling in Dover, but there must have been an awful lot of smuggling.

Photograph: Strange Cargo

On the Admiralty Pier, on that knuckle, there's a big dome, a massive great big dome. It's still in there now, and there's a massive, massive, massive gun in there. It's never been fired in anger, but they reckon if it was ever used in the war, they said it would have shattered every window in Dover when it went off. There was a big German warship that went by, the Bismarck, it went through the English Channel and it had all its guns trained on Dover. But the captain knew that that gun was trained on him, it was a bit of a stand off — if you fire on Dover, we'll fire this on you!

………………

There are two Armstrong 16 inch rifled muzzle-loading guns, each weighing 81 tons, within a circular cast-iron turret on Admiralty Pier. They're eight metres in length and could fire a 1,700-pound (771kg) shell nearly seven miles. They were never fired because by the time they were installed they were already old guns. Apparently, there was a proposal that the guns should be capable of blowing up the English end of the Channel Tunnel. That was in the days when plans for the undersea tunnel were for the exit to be near Shakespeare Beach.

Photograph: Mary Glow

Well, there's the Copt Hill Cemetery which is quite interesting. Lord Keyes of Zeebrugge is buried there. He masterminded the raid on Zeebrugge in 1918, which was a really big thing.

I don't know if he was born in Dover, but the man who invented the Flat Earth Society is also buried at Copt Hill Cemetery. It's a huge, sprawling burial ground that was originally known as Copt Hill Cemetery, but is now known as St James's.

Photograph: Rebecca Sperini

Fort Burgoyne is where all the Marines, the Navy, and that lot used to go onto the ships, and Nelson's ship you know, and all the ships that were coming into the harbour there; it was like the Marines' barracks up there.

The Grand Shaft was designed for whole regiments to be able to run down there at the same time, it's like a triple staircase. So they can all run down at once and if one falls over, they don't all fall over. So, if there was going to be a French invasion, they'd drop down, come running out and get across and run to the ships, and the ships would sail out. See, the Marines were always a part of the Navy.

Photograph: Susan Pilcher

Definitely, the beach is where young people just come and hang out in the summer, because you can all go in the sea and you've got an ice cream parlour just there, so yeah, perfect!

Photograph: Susan Pilcher

The first bomb dropped on Britain was dropped on Dover on Christmas Eve, 1914. There's a blue plaque on the wall of the house in Taswell Street where it fell.

The bomb made a large crater but only caused one casualty, Mr James Banks, a gardener who was slightly injured when he was knocked out of the tree he was pruning. Minimal damage was caused, with just a few broken windows. After the bombing, two British aeroplanes armed, it is said, with pistols, and a seaplane took off in pursuit, but failed to sight their quarry as it had vanished into clouds as it flew back to its Belgian airbase in Zeebrugge. Fragments of this bomb were mounted on a shield and presented to the King.

Photograph: Susan Pilcher

NEAR
THIS SPOT
ON
CHRISTMAS EVE 1914
FELL THE
FIRST AERIAL BOMB
EVER TO BE DROPPED
ON THE
UNITED KINGDOM

THE DOVER SOCIETY

You've got the military steps going up to the Drop Redoubt. Do you know the history of Drop Redoubt, the name? There are three versions:

1. You know the Roman Pharos at the top of the Castle? Well there was one at Western Heights too, but it's now just a bit of rubble. You have to go all the way up there to see it properly. They have open days up there, and it's called the 'Devil's Drop of Mortar'.

2. Another explanation is that it's where they used to hang the murderers.

3. The third story is a really great one: it's that the judge and jury and executioner were all the same person, who did the lot. They'd take the convicts up there and chuck them over the cliff!

....

The Drop Redoubt was built between 1804-8. A redoubt is a detached fort; the 'drop' refers to the remains of Dover's second Roman lighthouse, referred to locally as the 'Devil's Drop of Mortar'. The Pharos at Dover Castle is one of only three in the world to have survived from that time.

Photograph: Susan Pilcher

EVERYWHERE MEANS SOMETHING TO SOMEONE

Once you've navigated the route through to Dover seafront, it's quite an extraordinary place. On a sunny day, you'd be forgiven for thinking you were on the Continent. It's been recently refurbished and is beautifully laid out. It's never usually that busy and there are often swimmers training off the beach. There are lovely places to get a drink or an ice cream.

On the new Marina Curve, which was built on the site of the old Prince of Wales Pier, there are pop-ups serving street food and more traditional fare and, in sunnier weather, there's often live music playing there. There's a lovely, friendly café that is open all year called the Pedlar; it's popular with the locals and quite a trendy crowd go down there. Port of Dover is planning to build a big hotel at the end of the pier which will be a good local amenity, as Dover has lost much of its visitor accommodation over the years. The big building you can see is a temperature controlled multi-chamber warehouse, which stores all sorts of fresh produce. The solar panels on the roof means it's totally energy self-sufficient. It's the world's biggest ripening shed for bananas, melons and avocados and things like that.

The seafront's worth a visit — once you've found your way round there.

Photograph: Amy West

I can just recall the rebuilding of the seafront with those modern flats, and clearly remember the building and later destruction of the Dover Stage hotel between the new flats and the old Victorian parade. Another of our favourite places to explore was round Snargate Street and the original harbour alongside the long old rope shed; all of these places are in a book called *Dover Harbour* by Thomas Armstrong which is set in Napoleonic times, it's one of my favourite books and I would thoroughly recommend it.

Photograph: Susan Pilcher

We all went down to the Winter Light Up festival, and we were selling the uncollected lanterns to people without a lantern who wanted to join in the parade. We had to talk to people and get them involved, or the lanterns would have just gone in the bin.

Then we went down to Pencester and got some of the Future Foundry big Light Up lanterns, and we started walking down with the Mayor; me, Eleanor, Lincoln, Kai, Bradley and Poppy were all at the front, carrying lanterns for the parade. 'Cos the Mayor was there, obviously there were cameras, and then we had our photo taken loads of times. There's a photo of us outside Poundland walking in the road, and it ended up in the newspaper.

With the money we raised selling lanterns we had a Domino's party, so we ordered Domino's pizza for The Forge Christmas party and got to eat loads of pizza, and we still have money left over to do stuff in the future!

We spent 40 pounds, so we still have 35 left. We're gonna maybe use that money to do a little market, so maybe we can make more money.

Photograph: Matt Wilson / Future Foundry

EVERYWHERE MEANS SOMETHING TO SOMEONE

As a family we spent most of our Whitsun holiday breaks in the 50s staying on the seafront near the Eastern Docks at Mr and Mrs Ready's, of 24 Marine Parade. Mr Ready would take me up to the flat roof to collect gulls' eggs for breakfast, which to our surprise didn't taste of fish — they just had a very strong favour and deep yellow yolk colour.

I remember watching the old steamer ferries going in and out of the harbour, and there was a small engine which used to run along metal rails on the front, mainly delivering coal to the East Harbour from the Western Arm for the ferries, always with a man with a red flag walking in front of it. The rails are still there, just buried underneath the current pavement. Anyone with a metal detector would have a field day!

Photograph: Susan Pilcher

EVERYWHERE MEANS SOMETHING TO SOMEONE

My favourite view is when you stand on High Meadow — I'm going to award it my favourite view because not that many people get up there. High Meadow leads onto Whinless Down. High Meadow is actually the nearest place to the centre of town, but you have to go around the back. Once you get up there, you're on this side of Kearsney Abbey, and I do like that view of Dover Castle.

To me that's a special Dover place, more people should know it. You can look at the Castle and see the harbour and the sea, it's just a bit different. If it's in the summer you've got the horses wandering about, but there's so few people there. To me, that's special, so few hikers. You have to open the map out and really search — you'll find Whinless Down, but High Meadow is just at the end.

Photograph: Mary Glow

The crossroads in Dover, where Bridge Street, High Street and Tower Hamlets Road meet, there's a reminder that this is where criminals were hanged. The spot is marked with a blue plaque.

It was here that convicted criminals were hanged until 1823. Hanging days offered a great celebration for the rest of the town. Crowds gathered to watch the death, while expensive fees were charged to watch events from a window in a hotel overlooking the gallows.

The fellow to be hanged would have spent their last night in the town's prison in the Market Square, and then been carried in a horse-drawn cart through the main street to the place of execution. A number of smugglers, some from other towns, were left to swing by their necks here to warn others not to sin.

Photograph: Susan Pilcher

NEAR THIS SPOT
STOOD
DOVER'S
GALLOWS
WHERE
CRIMINALS WERE EXECUTED
BY HANGING
UNTIL 1823

SUPPORT
HIGHWAYMEN
ASHFORD

THE DOVER SOCIETY

My memories relate to the old ferry traffic in and out of the harbour, and the railway engine shunting coal wagons and coaches that ran along the seafront between the Eastern and Western Docks with a man with a red flag walking in front, and people helping to move and lift cars out of the way. There were small jetties that had signs saying 'trips around the harbour', and I remember my mother constantly removing tar from my trousers from sitting on the stony beach with the ever-present bottle of Thawpit in her handbag.

I recall regular walks along the promenade to the old Prince of Wales Pier, with the round and oddly-painted pink café at the end, and seeing the variety of fish that the anglers had caught. I remember having persuaded my parents to invest in some ice cream from the pagoda-roofed shops, which should keep us going on our way to Dover Marine Station to watch the Golden Arrow boat train arriving. Then visiting Shakespeare Beach via access across the railway lines controlled by an old railway footplate man who had lost a leg in the Second World War.

Photograph: Mary Glow

EVERYWHERE MEANS SOMETHING TO SOMEONE

The once-famous Lord Warden Hotel stands only a few yards from Shakespeare Beach, where many Channel swimmers start their attempts to swim to France. I believe it's owned by the Port of Dover.

The hotel, still well maintained, was built in 1853 as a railway centre where London train passengers could rest before crossing the Channel by ferry. It remained a top hotel until the start of the war in 1939, when it was taken over by the Royal Navy.

The building has seen much history. It was in this hotel where Napoleon III, Emperor of France, was reunited with his wife Eugenie on his exile to England in 1871. It was here that Louis Bleriot celebrated at a civic dinner after the first cross-Channel flight by an aircraft.

The hotel has hosted royalty, nobles, diplomats and writers, including Dickens and Thackeray, as they waited to cross the Channel. I think it's currently empty, but it was most recently used to accommodate import-export agents.

Photograph: Susan Pilcher

EVERYWHERE MEANS SOMETHING TO SOMEONE

LORD WARDEN HOTEL

1853–1939

NAPOLEON III

EMPEROR OF FRANCE
WAS REUNITED HERE
WITH HIS WIFE
EMPRESS EUGENIE
ON HIS EXILE
TO ENGLAND
1871.

THE DOVER SOCIETY

One of England's top tourist attractions is the White Cliffs of Dover. But the clifftops would have been pock-marked with derelict rusty buildings if a 20th century mine owner had realised his ambitions.

Richard Tilden Smith owned a coal mine near Dover, and sought markets that would buy his coal. His ambitious plans came in during a laissez faire era, with few planning restrictions. He decided to establish steel manufacturing at an easy distance from Tilmanstone Colliery. He argued that it would be cheaper to create electrical power for the steel works near his coal production. He also realised there were many by-products available from the coal being mined in East Kent. He leased several acres of farmland at the top of the cliffs, east of the Port of Dover, and sought financial backers for his proposals for the steel works, tar manufacturing, and a large cement factory, using the million tons of chalk available from the white cliffs.

Tilden's drastic industrial proposals came to a halt with his sudden death in 1929, following a hearty lunch at the House of Commons. Just imagine, if his plans had gone ahead, what a mess the White Cliffs would be in today.

Photograph: Rebecca Sperini

EVERYWHERE MEANS SOMETHING TO SOMEONE

The Dour is a chalk stream, which is very rare, there are only 200 in the world. It's the reason Dover is located where it is. It used to be a really busy river. It's only four miles long, and it used to have 13 watermills along its route. It boasts one of the few operational water mills in Kent at Crabble. It also has its own 'water locked' population of brown trout, and you can even spot water voles along the banks.

....

Until I was ten we lived in Beresford Road in River. We had the River Dour running at the bottom of our garden. My dad was a keen fly fisherman, and he had a licence to fish there. As a kid I also used to try to catch tadpoles from the steps that Dad had built going down to the river; it was all quite dangerous really. We used to feed the ducks that used to come into our garden — Muscovy and Mandarin ducks were regular visitors.

Photograph: Amy West

There's a semi-detached house in Dover which, for a number of crucial wartime months, was the nation's only weather station. I doubt if the residents of 70 Stanhope Road realise the unique history of their house.

During the Second World War the broadcasting of weather conditions or forecasts was banned, in case the details helped enemy bombers. But, in the summer of 1940, with enemy forces on the Calais cliffs, Hitler and his generals could see what the weather was like in southern England. The issue was raised in Parliament, with the Home Office agreeing to allow publication only of weather conditions in the English Channel.

Fleet Street newspapers jumped at the opportunity. But who was going to do it? They turned to the only Dover-based wartime journalist, Norman Sutton. Twice a day, Norman would venture out into his Stanhope Road garden, tap his barometer and thermometer, study the clouds, and phone the results through to the newspapers. Many wartime front pages, still available today, carried a paragraph resulting from Norman's part-time work. His unique position as the UK's wartime weatherman was confirmed in his obituary in *The Times*.

Photograph: Rebecca Sperini

Once, there was a time when there were plenty of film stars passing through. One night I spent time at Dover Docks with the famous Brigitte Bardot. It wasn't at all romantic.

As a journalist, I was tipped off that the French actress and the film director Roger Vadim were filming a sequence at the train ferry dock (now gone) at the Western Docks. I had no difficulty boarding the train ferry, had a short chat with the French film crew, and asked where I could find Brigitte.

Co-star Jane Birkin came to my rescue, and pointed to a female on the deck. It was Bardot, crying, her tears running down her face mixing with mascara. I didn't get much of a quote from Brigitte, but it made a few lines in some of the Fleet Street newspapers for whom I then worked. And made me a lifetime fan of Jane Birkin.

Photograph: Strange Cargo

EVERYWHERE MEANS SOMETHING TO SOMEONE

I don't know lots, but in 2012 our house burnt down. That was, like, 12 years ago, and we've been in the house for 10 or 11 years and moved into a brand-new version of the house after it had burnt down. My house is not haunted, but we don't know why it burnt down.

It was previously owned by my mum's friend's great, great grandfather, and it had, like, maids and a big spiral staircase and it had a *Downton Abbey* vibe. It had lots of other people live there after, but then it burnt down, and we now live in the newer version of it. I found out because when my mum was coming home, we bumped into the friend who told us the story and we were like, "Woah, no way!"

Photograph: Susan Pilcher

EVERYWHERE MEANS SOMETHING TO SOMEONE

LONDON ROAD

When my family would holiday in Dover in the 1950s, my sister and I would invariably try to make a raft from all the flotsam and jetsam washed up on the beach. We even found a toilet door (it still said 'engaged') and seat which we decorated with old shoes, bits of rope, seaweed, rusting tins, cork floats etc, and set afloat.

Photograph: Susan Pilcher

Snargate Street, overlooking the Docks, was once Dover's top commercial centre. Here stood the big houses of the wealthy. One of the biggest was the birthplace of Philip Yorke in 1690, who later was appointed as the nation's Lord Chancellor as Baron Hardwicke.

Yorke played an important role developing something which is still part of everyday life in today's world: the calling of Banns of Marriage in churches. Before he became Lord Chancellor there were many examples of men forcing wealthy girls into marriage, so the new husband could control her wealth. Fake clergymen were available to carry out the traditional wedding ceremony. Yorke put an end to this practice by forcing through Parliament the 1753 Marriage Act, which included the calling of banns. Today, with Snargate Street a slice of the A20, it is a very different place to Yorke's time.

....

You know Snargate Street, on the front in Dover? Well behind there, in the cliffs, are old wine cellars. It's not publicly accessible, but they go way back into the cliff. We sometimes do a guided walk based on characters from Dover, as we've had our share of very interesting characters.

Photograph: Rebecca Sperini

EVERYWHERE MEANS SOMETHING TO SOMEONE

The Market Square, where once Roman galleys rode at anchor, has for centuries been the hub of Dover life, and it was here where those who broke the law received harsh punishment. Here were based the town's stocks, pillory, whipping post and cage. Men and women were often whipped here before being exiled from the town. Women who were caught being too free with their bodies were, at times, stripped to the waist, tied to a horse-drawn cart and whipped out of town. One convicted pickpocket was nailed by his ear to the pillory and told he could go free once he had cut his own ear off.

Leading off Market Square is Gaol Lane: a pedestrian-only lane next to the museum. Dover's prison existed here for many years. After a riot in 1820, Folkestone smugglers broke in and released their friends. The lane is now partially occupied by Dover's community cinema.

....

I was sitting in a café in Market Square one day and the chap behind the counter told me that the lines of black paving slabs in Market Square show where the foundations of Roman buildings are located under the modern square.

Photograph: Mary Glow

EVERYWHERE MEANS SOMETHING TO SOMEONE

Today, the former Marine Station is a quiet, eerie place. But once it was a frantic scene of trains, steam and smoke, with luggage porters rushing between the London boat trains and the ferries. Royalty, diplomats, millionaires, film and stage stars and a few rogues passed through. It was here where blood-stained Hungarian refugees arrived after street fighting with Russian invaders.

As a journalist I would wait there, watched by the railway police. Among those I was able to welcome to England were Humphrey Bogart and Lauren Bacall, who posed for me to take a picture. Bob Hope was another. Not so pleasant was my 'hero' Rex Harrison, who I had always admired. He had suffered a rough Channel crossing, had had far too much to drink, and had experienced a difficult time with Customs. He thought I had been sent by his studio to pick him up. His wife, trailing behind, was burdened with luggage, so I offered to help.

Harrison turned on me, threatened to punch me, insisted I leave his wife to carry the luggage and to bring the studio car round. The threat of violence was too much. I told him to get lost (or words to that effect) and left him fuming on the station's platform. Rex was no longer my hero.

Photograph: Strange Cargo

EVERYWHERE MEANS SOMETHING TO SOMEONE

Here is my story about being an extra in the film *The War Game*.

The Grand Shaft Barracks were demolished shortly after the film was made; however, the weird Grand Shaft staircase survives and is a listed building owned by Dover District Council and managed by the Western Heights Preservation Society, which has a key.

I was a guinea-a-day extra in Peter Watkins' film. The film documents events leading up to a nuclear attack on a Medway town and subsequent civil unrest. Many of the action sequences were filmed at the Grand Shaft Barracks using local people, including teachers and school kids like me who found it great fun. I shot my history master Mr Dale for food rioting. We blazed away but then got told off by the film's armourer for wasting valuable ammunition. The film was banned in 1965 by the BBC because of its horrific content. It later won an Oscar and was widely shown by CND. The drama critic Kenneth Tynan described it as the most important film ever made.

Photograph: Amy West

Every time I see this from the window of my bus, I try to imagine a scenario in which a tank trap from the Second World War ends up adorning the front garden of a terraced house.

I did some research concerning this anti-tank obstacle. They were called dragons' teeth, and were designed to prevent tanks from passing over them. They had substantial foundations and were made of solid concrete, so it is most unlikely this one was put there for aesthetic reasons. I assume that they were installed in 1940-41 as part of plans to thwart Operation Sealion — the invasion of southern England. The Germans were intending to land an army at Dover harbour. Capturing Buckland Bridge, where the road to London crosses the river Dour, would have been an early objective, and Hillside Road is located on the hill overlooking that river crossing. However, this is guesswork. It is probably best to consult a local archaeologist with an interest in Second World War structures in and around Dover on all matters connected with the military.

Photograph: Rebecca Sperini

In Pencester Gardens there's a children's park that you can take your kids to, and there's the skate park for scooters and skateboards and bikes and stuff with metal ramps. It just got refurbished, with new concrete at the bottom. They're good ramps, not quite the best, but still pretty good. There's quite a few Dover skaters, mainly older.

There were more new skaters after Christmas, who got new boards and stuff. A lot of people skate in the summer, but don't come out in the winter. We sometimes go to Deal to skate; there's Folkestone 51, the multi-storey one; Hythe has one too, so there's quite a lot of places. I'm pretty sure they have a park in Capel, but I've never skated there. It's free to skate in Dover.

Photograph: Rebecca Sperini

EVERYWHERE MEANS SOMETHING TO SOMEONE

The Lord Nelson was here at least 60 years before I was on the planet, and was my first watering hole, before the whole St James's development. There was a bus station and TV studios there before it was developed, and my friend used to work in there, so I visited a few times. They'd broadcast the local news, stuff like that. There was a multistorey carpark opposite the Nelson, the oldest pub in Kent.

The White Horse pub, pretty much everybody that's swum the Channel has signed their name in there over the years. Most pubs have disappeared. There was The Eagle when I first started at Sainsbury's in 1980. I grew up in Elms Vale; there are still two pubs at one end of the road to the other, The Crown and Sceptre and The Bull's Head, they have live music. There are some superb musicians in this town. You've got The Hind in Market Square, and The Bull at the end of London Road at the other end of town. The Louis Armstrong is still going, and was one of my first musical experiences at 15, playing drums, bass guitar and singing with my band The Golden Wonders.

Photograph: Rebecca Sperini

EVERYWHERE MEANS SOMETHING TO SOMEONE

I used to do all sorts of gardening, I loved lots of types of plants, the evergreens especially. I planted a big cherry tree in memory of my mum when she passed away, it's something to look at every day. It's big now, it's been growing for over 20 years. We've trimmed it back lots of times, as we have to make sure the roots don't come under the house and do any damage.

Gardening is so relaxing; you can get so cooped up inside. On our road we have a pretty blue flowers that creep up everywhere, lifting up the coping on garden walls. What's it called? Campanula, that's it. The roots get under everything. When it's in bloom it's beautiful and stops other weeds from growing. The frost doesn't kill it.

We used to do a lot of gardening together, but we can't now. We have a lilac tree which was there when we moved in, 54 years ago now. It's starting to fall apart now. Something got in it and is eating it. It was there before we moved in, so were the roses. They've lived such a long time.

Photograph: Rebecca Sperini

EVERYWHERE MEANS SOMETHING TO SOMEONE

I came to Dover for love. I do notice when there's new people in town, who've arrived here for whatever reason. There's always some lost souls, and men who are trying to find their way back from a broken heart.

The amount of males there are in East Kent who come here for reasons of the heart.

I was speaking to someone recently who has played drums on some of the most famous musicians' albums, and we got chatting and I asked him, what brings an American to East Kent, and he said, "There was this gal!"

Photograph: Rebecca Sperini

David Copperfield was said to have sat on that step. David Copperfield was down in Dover looking for his Aunt Betsy Trotwood and he couldn't find her. He was on his uppers, and he was sitting on that step, that one there, and a horseman went past and dropped a cloth or something and David picked it up and handed it back to the horseman and said, "Do you know my Great Aunt? I'm looking for my Great Aunt Betsy Trotwood," and the horseman said, "Ah, she lives on the seafront in an upturned boat." So, Charles Dickens must have been here in Dover looking at that step at some stage.

Photograph: Rebecca Sperini

EVERYWHERE MEANS SOMETHING TO SOMEONE

This little building is three times lucky. It's survived Henry VIII's Dissolution of the Monasteries, then the war, then the council's road widening scheme. It's the smallest church in England in regular use.

The Maison Dieu existed because pilgrims were coming from all over to Canterbury to visit the tomb of St Thomas Becket. They all used to go up to the Priory here and the monks couldn't cope, so they created a hospice, a place where pilgrims could rest overnight or get help if needed. St Edmund's was built as a cemetery chapel.

There is a collection of beautiful, rounded pebbles with holes in them on the altar, and it's suggested that the pilgrims hunted around on the beach for offerings, pebbles they thought they were lucky I suppose, and they brought them here.

St Richard of Chichester, who consecrated this chapel in the name of his good friend St Edmund of Abingdon, died in the hospice three days after he'd done the consecration, and needed to be carted back to Chichester. But they couldn't take his whole body, so it's said they cut out bits off him and put them under the altar in a chest, so bits of him are said to be down there.

Photograph: Amy West

EVERYWHERE MEANS SOMETHING TO SOMEONE

It took the Romans 200 years to conquer Britain; we must have put up a good fight, and the making it difficult started here in Dover. When they eventually did make the conquest, Dover was obviously a pivotal point for the Romans coming in and going all over the country. So, it was a strategic area, but from what I've read, it was not a popular place for the Roman soldiers to be billeted: it was a long way from home, a horrible climate to what they were used to in Italy, and generally it was a place they didn't want to come to. So, effectively, what the Romans did was build a glamorous hotel in Dover, so when the officers came, who were probably all moaning, they could have this hotel where they could be pampered and made a fuss of and made to feel it was worth their while.

What remains is one tiny wing, and that's the Roman Painted House. What you've got there is actual Roman plaster with paintings of Bacchus, wine and grapes, and the sort of stuff you'd associate with Rome. It's all in colour, which is still preserved. I'm sure it's the only example in Britain and one of the few in the world.

Photograph: Strange Cargo

EVERYWHERE MEANS SOMETHING TO SOMEONE

The Golden Arrow train was a luxury boat train in the days before roll-on, roll-off ferries. It travelled from London to Dover, where passengers boarded a ferry to Calais. Then they transferred to the French Fleche d`Or which took them to Paris. The service started in 1929, using the *Canterbury* for the ferry crossing. The train consisted of Pullman cars.

There was no service during the Second World War from September 1939. The service resumed in April 1946. A different ferry, the *Invicta* was now used. A new set of Pullman coaches was built in 1951. In 1961, an electrically-hauled service was introduced, but competition from other forms of transport saw a decline in demand for rail travel between London and Paris. The last Golden Arrow ran on 30th September 1972.

It was the last train to use Dover Marine Station in 1994, and has featured on Royal Mail stamps. A steam locomotive pulled Golden Arrow Pullman cars at the inauguration of the Channel Tunnel.

However, to keep the memory alive, steam trains such as the *Braunton* in the photograph still travel the route using Pullman cars and displaying the two flags.

Photograph: Tony Poole

I used to canvas the area a lot, and Clarendon Place claims to be Kent's longest terraced street. When Clarendon Place becomes Clarendon Road, you go by all these late Victorian houses there, but every so often there's a gap, like a missing tooth for want of a better word, and in the gap there are more modern houses. That apparently is where doodlebugs hit the town. Dover had a rough time in the Second World War.

Photograph by Susan Pilcher

We're talking the 80s now, and we used to go over to Calais regularly as foot passengers for a 'booze cruise'. Relatives used to stay with us, and we'd all trip on the step and break a few bottles on the way home. They were pretty unruly times; there wasn't a lot of security for people who got on the boat. You could buy a Sealink ticket and return on a Townsend Thoresen and nobody would really realise.

I never saw any unpleasantness, but people were really loud when they were enjoying themselves. This wouldn't happen today, but my brother-in-law came regularly to stay with us to go across on the ferry. On one such occasion he came down from Bedford and had forgotten his passport; I said never mind they don't look too closely, just take my wife's passport and if they stop us we'll just say that when you got up this morning you picked hers up by mistake. It sounded like a good idea, so that's what he did. When you went through the passports, it wasn't single file, you just went through en masse and waved your passport about. So, we did that, got through, had our day, no problems at all!

Photograph: Susan Pilcher

This café really shows the best of Dover. It evolved from a soup kitchen, and fundamentally it's a normal café which provides drinks, food, and breakfast. Anyone can come in and buy food or a drink, but if someone comes and genuinely can't afford it, they can get it for nothing or a reduced fee. When people like myself are using it we're encouraged to make a donation if possible. I don't know if you like Americanos, but this genuinely is the best Americano in town, hands down!

Photograph: Strange Cargo

At the 1994 Dover Pageant, the last one at Connaught Park, the Mayor of Deal and the Mayor of Dover challenged each other in a chariot race, one Mayor on each chariot. They were warned: bicycle wheels go straight, do not try to cut someone off, or something like that. The chariots were fast, they were each pulled by four rugby players, and the Mayor of Deal just got carried away, saw the Mayor of Dover was pulling away and told her lads to cut them off and over she went, and the Chain of Office hit her right in the head and she was out cold!

We had St John's Ambulance there, and they rushed on, and when she came to she said, "Oh, what a silly billy I am. I should have listened!" Luckily she didn't sue, but it did bring up health and safety, and that was the end of the chariot races, as I could see how dangerous it was. The Pageant moved back to Dover College after that.

Photograph: Amy West

The *Admiral Day* dredger changed its name to the *David Church*. He was a Harbour Board fellow who arranged the dredging side of the business; when he passed away they renamed the ship after him. They used to bring it up, and the tugboats, and the *Diana*... all the Harbour Board working ships were brought up on that slip, which is now just a wall. You can see it went the full length of the carpark, and they blocked it off. There was a big motor room, and they'd cable the ship on, put it up on green timbers and rollers, and then winch it in like that — when the tide went down this big motor would pull the ship up. They would chock it all up and give it a complete refurb, take all the shells off the bottom, all the clinkers, and then completely anti-foul it and do all the work that needed to be done. Once De Bradelei was built, it was decommissioned and they stopped doing that type of work. Now they send ships abroad, or further up the line. It's a shame really, because Dover had its own dry dock. It couldn't take massive ships, but it took good size work boats.

Photograph: Strange Cargo

I was watching the television and found out we'd won the Olympics, and it got me thinking that it wouldn't be a bad idea if we had a pre-Olympics archery competition here in Dover. So I went to the Mayor and asked if I could have a room and invite all the key players in archery, and I put it to them that we could stage an archery competition. Someone at that meeting then met with the Grand National Archery Association, who mentioned that they'd lost their venue for the next European Championship, so he said, "There's a guy down in Dover who'd like to do something."

So, they rang me up and I offered to show them three venues: "You're the experts, you tell me if they're suitable." The second place I showed them was the Duke of York's, and I took them through to the playing fields and they said, "This is amazing, it's better than our national facilities." A fortnight later they phoned and said we have a problem, we want to upgrade it from the European to the World Archery Championship. That's how it went, and so Dover hosted the 2007 World Archery Championship.

Photograph: Susan Pilcher

I was talking to the Brigadier up at the Castle and I said, "You represent the Queen, don't you?" See, it was the Queen's Jubilee coming up. He replied, "Yes," and I said, "Wouldn't it be nice if we brought back the Military Tattoo that Dover used to have?" We were a military town, and we used to put this amazing Military Tattoo on. The Brigadier said, "That's not bad idea, give me a bit of time."

He came back with funding, and I negotiated to get Connaught Barracks for £1. I then booked the White Helmets, and I booked the parachutes and started to have site meetings. Unfortunately, the White Helmets and parachutes said, "Sorry mate, it's a bit small for us, there's not enough room." So we had to move the whole event across to the parade ground and it was very successful — the only downside was the Australian who did a parachute jump: as he came past the stand, he took the wind out of his parachute and he came down *boff* and broke 11 bones. He actually made contact with me about a month after and said he wanted to do it again!

Photograph: Susan Pilcher

There's a fairly quiet spot on the promenade near the clock tower, at the western end of the prom, that marks a very important date in British history.

Near this spot, on Dover beach, Charles II landed on the Restoration of the Monarchy in 1660. His arrival on 29th May is today celebrated as Oak Apple Day.

He was welcomed back to his homeland by General Monck, who had demanded the dissolution of Cromwell's Parliament, leading to the Restoration. The Mayor of Dover was on the beach to welcome Charles ashore.

Charles II lived on until 1685, when his brother became King as James VII of Scotland and James II of England.

Photograph: Strange Cargo

EVERYWHERE MEANS SOMETHING TO SOMEONE

CAMDEN CRESCENT

A blue plaque in Camden Crescent celebrates the life of Cuthbert Ottaway, the first man to captain an England football team in the very first international match. Born in Hammond Place in July 1850, a stone's throw from St James's parish church, Cuthbert was the only child of James, a surgeon, JP and former Mayor of Dover, and Jane, sister of Sir John Bridge.

With the family relocated to Camden Crescent, Cuthbert was sent on a scholarship to Eton School and later to Brasenose College, Oxford. While at Oxford, Cuthbert represented the University at five different sports, including athletics and rackets, even captaining the University team in their 2-0 defeat of The Royal Engineers in the 1874 FA Cup Final.

Ottaway also excelled at cricket, both with the bat and as a wicket keeper, first representing Kent aged 19. Cuthbert went on to tour with, effectively, an England representative side and once shared a 150-run partnership with W G Grace, widely considered, even now, as one of the sport's greatest players. Ottaway qualified as a barrister in November 1876 and married Canadian-born Marion Stinson in August 1877. Sadly, only eight months later, Cuthbert Ottaway died from pneumonia aged 28.

Photograph: Rebecca Sperini

EVERYWHERE MEANS SOMETHING TO SOMEONE

I have a picture in my hall of a carriage coming down Castle Street with a Household Cavalry escort, and there's only one thing that it could be: when the Queen Mother was installed as Lord Warden of the Cinque Ports. The position is vacant at the moment, but it dates back at least to the 12th century. It is a prestigious position: we've had Sir Winston Churchill, Sir Robert Menzies, The Queen Mother and, most recently, Lord Boyce. The Lord Warden is traditionally invested here in Dover.

Photograph: Susan Pilcher

EVERYWHERE MEANS SOMETHING TO SOMEONE

Whenever I pass 12 Athol Terrace, I look at the framed and fading copy of Matthew Arnold's poem *Dover Beach* mounted on the wall by the front door and reflect on my school days, which were in Bath, not Dover. My English teacher, Mrs Rosamund Rhymes, told us that Matthew Arnold was an ancestor of hers, I think a great or great, great uncle.

The physical erosion of the printed poem by the elements seems to fittingly echo not only Arnold's words about a place where 'you hear the grating roar of pebbles...', but also my gradually dimming memories of half a century ago.

Photograph: Susan Pilcher

On a winter's evening alone in my storage room at Lord Warden House, with an easterly wind moaning through the corridors, I think of the ghost story writer M R James, who often stayed here when it was a railway hotel. The penultimate scene of his story *Casting the Runes* takes place in one of the rooms — possibly my room, with its faint coal dust smell.

'Long and long the two sat in their room at the Lord Warden... Had they been justified in sending a man to his death, as they believed they had?'

....

Lord Warden House opened in 1853, connected by a glazed walkway at first floor level to the Town Station and the Admiralty Pier, where the cross-Channel steamers berthed. The hotel was designed by Samuel Beazley, architect, novelist and playwright, who was the leading theatre architect of his time. He designed, or substantially redesigned, seven London theatres including the Lyceum and the Theatre Royal, Drury Lane. The hotel attracted a clientele from the rich and famous en route to and from the Continent. Charles Dickens was a guest, as was William Makepeace Thackeray. In March 1871 the deposed Emperor Napoleon III of France arrived to be reunited with his wife Eugenie here.

Photograph: Susan Pilcher

EVERYWHERE MEANS SOMETHING TO SOMEONE

Just outside the walls of Dover Castle, at Northfall Meadow, there's a historic site marked out in the shape of an early aeroplane.

In July 1909, French aviator Louis Bleriot (1872-1930) became the first person to successfully fly an aircraft across the English Channel. He set off near Calais and landed at what was then a treeless meadow at Northfall, Dover. His crossing time was 36 minutes and 30 seconds. Hundreds of people flocked to the meadow to see Bleriot's fragile aircraft, and as they crowded around it they trampled the grass down. This gave the editor of the *Dover Express* newspaper the idea to permanently mark out the aircraft's landing spot. The idea was taken up nationally so, in time, it was paved with concrete slabs which remain today. But no longer is Northfall Meadow treeless. Vegetation has taken over, with trees and undergrowth crowding in on the historic site, but a way is kept clear for visitors through the wooded area to Bleriot's landing spot.

....

In 1909, Bleriot landed on the wrong cliff. There was a postcard produced in advance, showing the landing, but it shows the wrong cliff, by Dover Castle. There's a statue of him on the seafront.

Photograph: Mary Glow

I saw Barry from *Eastenders* in Dover. He turned the Christmas lights on in, I think it was 2003, which was a pretty peak time for his character. He was wearing a black faux leather jacket, dressed pretty much as his character.

Photograph: Mary Glow

There is an amazing little hidden walk and a bridge from Aycliffe to Shakespeare Beach. It's so cool, it's easy to cross from the town and I think it's the only sandy beach in Dover; it's like your own private beach. If you're coming from the beach front, you need to walk past Admiralty Pier, over Shakespeare's main stony beach. It's a good 10 to 15 minute walk on stones, you have to climb down a rocky bit, but it's totally worth it. The views. The chalk cliff. I have great memories of cockle picking with my grandad there, but you have to watch out for chalk falling. We have a bench there for my grandad, he always wanted to be there.

Photograph: Mary Glow

EVERYWHERE MEANS SOMETHING TO SOMEONE

In the centre of Dover, next to the bus terminal, is Pencester Gardens, named after the Norman knight Stephen de Pencester. It's normally a quiet spot with the river Dour flowing by. But at one stage in its history, when the land was just a meadow, there were proposals to make this the entrance to the dreamed-of Channel Tunnel. Just imagine the town centre traffic congestion if that idea had gone ahead!

Pencester Gardens, now owed and looked after by Dover District Council, was controversially purchased as a meadow by Dover Borough Council. There were those who argued it was a waste of rate payers' money. Then, as the purchase went through, it was discovered the seller of the meadow did not own as much of it as stated in the contract.

During the 1939-45 war, an air raid shelter slit trench was cut into the lawns, and the garden became the base for a barrage balloon, sent aloft to protect Dover against enemy dive bombers.

Photograph: Mary Glow

High on the slopes above Dover there was, before the Reformation, a hospital where few dared to venture. St Bartholomew's Hospital for Lepers was established by two monks from St Martin's Priory and was located on Chapel Hill, off Buckland Terrace and London Road — the road takes its name from the hospital's chapel.

Dover, as a busy seaport, had to make provision for travellers suffering from leprosy arriving in the town. In the 13th century there were nearly 2,000 leper hospitals in Europe. Those were the days when Dover people were warned when a leper was approaching. He or she had to give warning with a clapper or a bell while walking in the town. There was a dreaded fear that getting near a leper would result in catching the disease.

According to documents kept in the Bodleian Library in Oxford, the religious community running the leper hospital in Dover consisted of eight Brothers and Sisters of Mercy suffering from leprosy. Rules for the lepers at St Bartholomew's demanded they behaved themselves, not play pranks by knocking on doors — especially doors leading to the women's sleeping areas — and the women were instructed not to make dates with the menfolk.

Photograph: Strange Cargo

One of a number of statues and monuments on Dover seafront is a bust of Captain Matthew Webb, the first person to have swum the English Channel. He made the crossing from Dover to France in August 1875 in nearly 22 hours.

However, if he made the same start-to-finish crossing today, Webb's swim would not be officially recognised by the Channel Swimming Association. Their rules state that to be successful, a swimmer must have no sea between the swimmer and the shore. They must start from the beach and crawl, or walk, up the opposite beach — Webb started his historic swimming by jumping off Dover pier. Of course, there were no rules at that stage.

Captain Webb, a national hero, died in July 1883 trying to swim across the rapids of the Niagara Falls. His body was located seven miles down river.

Photograph: Mary Glow

The majority of the land from the A20 to the harbourside is officially looked after by Dover Harbour Board; they are the custodians of this space, and it's owned by Port of Dover. There are a few pockets that have some other ownership, but generally Port of Dover owns the land.

The Eastern Docks is where the ferry operation takes place, and there have been lots of changes in its lifetime. During the war it was taken over by the War Department. There are tunnels here that have huge fuel berths, tanks which are actually enormous. The fuel was used by the Dover Patrol which was the fleet tasked with trying to protect the Channel.

Every year the town commemorates the historic Zeebrugge Raid on the 6th of March. The flag from the ship is in the Dover Town Council building.

Photograph: Rebecca Sperini

From the coach park opposite Dover Castle, face east and you're looking directly onto what was once the site of Dover Golf Club. Founded in 1890, the 10-hole course measured a total of 2,540 yards (2.3km) and featured such hazards as '...a terrifying chalk pit, a farmyard, and ramparts of a fort.'

Having been damaged by protesting suffragettes in 1913, the following year it was taken over by the United Services Golf Club and was closed, only reopening to the public in 1928 when the War Office agreed to transfer the lease. With the agreement of the military authorities, play resumed that September, with the first tee located at the top of Castle Hill, conveniently close to the bus stop, and construction of a pavilion nearby started in the October.

Used for grazing purposes during the Second World War, it was not until 1946 that the committee held a meeting to consider reviving the golf club as an 18-hole course. In May 1947 the War Office advised that, in light of the ongoing national emergency and the country's agricultural needs, they could only approve a nine-hole course. The proposition was unacceptable to the committee so, in 1948, the Dover Golf Club ceased to exist.

Photograph: Rebecca Sperini

EVERYWHERE MEANS SOMETHING TO SOMEONE

For centuries, many Dover folk lived in caves carved out of the cliffs. Some caves were used for storage, to keep food cool or to hide smuggled goods. But a cave could be a fatal trap. John Poole, a 48-year-old master carpenter lived with his large family at East Cliff in the shadow of the high cliff. They used their cave partly as a piggery.

On the night of 14th December 1810 there was a huge rock fall onto the Pooles' home. It killed John's wife Eliza Poole and six children, aged six to 13. By some miracle, John Poole escaped with injuries.

But what about the family pig in the cave piggery? Rescuers dug through the fallen chalk and, in May the following year, the animal was discovered to be alive. The fat pig had survived for 160 days but, according to reports, it was unable to walk and looked like a skeleton, but it lived on.

Photograph: Mary Glow

It's kind of Dover, but maybe not really Dover, but it's still a really cool story. There's this place called Chef De Mumbai, it's an Indian restaurant on Deal Road.

There's this experience me and my dad had; we both experienced it together. We work together and do nightshifts — I work as a waitress and finish at, like, 11pm sometimes if its busy. We both saw ghosts, we saw soldiers — we could see their uniforms. They were walking in and out, in and out, inside the building, right in front of us. They were almost marching through doors. It was probably the best experience I have ever had.

We tried to film it on our phones, but you can't see it on there. It was scary but cool. It felt like they were under us in the basement too.

There's actually an old airfield nearby, so it sort of makes sense.

Photograph: Susan Pilcher

It was built as a Turkish bath house in 1881, you can still see the bath area under the floorboards. After some reincarnations it's been reborn as a venue and arts space. It's amazing, there's always something going on: exhibitions, Pride planning, makers' markets, workshops, queer cabaret, youth projects, music groups, a club house for young people to just come along and be themselves. There are so many unique and beautiful people involved in Biggin Hall, it's a hub of diversity, it's a magical space where all things are possible.

....

The Turkish baths used to be public when I was a kid; a lot of the houses didn't have a bath so you could go there. This was many years ago. Most of the houses would not have had modern sanitation... well, they would have had outside toilets, but no hot water. Some didn't have electricity. You had your larder, your toilet and then your shed. I can remember big queues outside, people with towels around their necks, and no disrespect, they weren't down-and-outs down there, it was for anyone that wanted to have a bath. I mean we only bathed once a week, Sunday night, that was the night. Nit comb through the hair.

Photograph: Mary Glow

EVERYWHERE MEANS SOMETHING TO SOMEONE

RIVER DOUR TRAIL

I was always going to retire to East Kent, to go to the seaside. I have friends nearby. When the time came to move, I decided to visit all the towns, from Margate to Hythe. And, to my great surprise, I loved Dover.

I was incredibly lucky, it was purely by chance. I was doing a box-ticking exercise. I thought I will go, I won't just write it off. I was able to buy a slightly better house, but that was just a bonus at the time.

I came to view a house on Crabble Hill, and then I thought, oh I'll walk back. I went round Kearsney and back on the river Dour trail, through River and round the back. I got to Buckland Bridge and when you're there, up comes the Castle, then down the river, past graffiti and art, and then you go into the town and past Pencester Gardens and out to the seafront. I thought, this is a lovely place! What are people going on about?

That is probably the best walk here, and it was purely a fluke that I found it that day. When you go from River round to Buckland it's flat, and you can cycle it.

Photograph: Rebecca Sperini

EVERYWHERE MEANS SOMETHING TO SOMEONE

Few realise that a king of England died in Dover. It was in 1154 when King Stephen was in Dover trying to secure the aid of foreign troops to reinstate him to the throne.

Stephen was crowned King in 1135. He was in dispute with Empress Matilda and, in 1138, Matilda's troops invaded from the north. Stephen lost the battle of 1141 and was imprisoned, but he was released by his supporters, causing Matilda to flee. Fighting continued, resulting in Stephen travelling to Dover to seek foreign military aid. He spent the night of 25th October 1154 at Dover Priory, now the site of Dover College, where he died. His remains were removed from Dover to an abbey which had been founded by his wife at Faversham.

Stephen was succeeded by Henry II, the first of the Plantagenet monarchs.

....

There's a St Thomas of Dover. Thomas Hales served as a Benedictine Monk at St Martin's Priory, now Dover Priory. Thomas refused to tell a French raiding party in 1295 where the silver was in the Priory, so he was killed. Tales of miracles were reported at his tomb, and he was later made a saint by King Richard II.

Photograph: Mary Glow

EVERYWHERE MEANS SOMETHING TO SOMEONE

Having worked on a couple of coastal town regeneration projects, I was asked to scope the Market Square for the prospect of entertainment and events following its renovation. On a sunny day, just as lockdown was lifting, I walked around the empty square, looking at the angles. Pubs and shops were still shut, but KFC was open, so I treated myself to a cheeky Colonel Sanders.

Sat on the old, low wooden benches in the sun, dripping ketchup down my full lockdown beard, I was approached by a solitary cyclist who stopped beside me. "Are you enjoying it?" he asked. "The sun?" I replied, looking up at him shielding my eyes from the sun, like an incomer in a Spaghetti Western, "or the KFC?" "Dover" he said. "Oh, yes, I come over here quite a lot, for work and stuff," I nodded. "You don't live here, then?" "Well, no, I actually live in Folkestone," I said. He paused. "So why don't you clear off (or words to that effect) back to Folkestone, then?" he replied, cycling off and flicking me a V-sign, accompanied by a raspberry. Was it my beard, I wondered... or the beret?

A year later we put on a vintage dance event where people danced the conga around the new water feature.

Photograph: Peter Cocks

If you're driving towards London, before you head uphill out of town, cast your eyes seaward, and you'll see what looks like the ghost of a grand hotel and a Cenotaph-like structure almost floating out at sea.

Wheeling left and past the old harbour stop, past lorry parks, containers, and a dockside pub you'll arrive at Dover Marine Station. Monumental, classically detailed, your eyes will widen as you enter, finding yourself in a mostly abandoned station of the quality of London Marylebone... in the sea. Like a microcosm of Englishness as imagined by a foreign tourist, Dover Marine Station boasts brick-built waiting rooms, red telephone boxes, and war memorials. Pale light filters through the glazed roof, throwing buttresses, rivets and cast ironmongery into sharp relief.

At the far end, the Cruise Terminal transfers tourists onto coaches to Canterbury for shopping, avoiding the Marine Station altogether. One Christmas, the Port of Dover set up a market with stalls and an ice rink; food and drink concessions took over waiting rooms, the air full of candy floss, mulled wine and roasting chestnuts, music and chatter. For a golden moment, Dover Marine Station came to life again and then, like Brigadoon, disappeared into a colourful memory of barrel organs, fun and vapour.

Photograph: Strange Cargo

EVERYWHERE MEANS SOMETHING TO SOMEONE

When you're standing in the entrance of the remains of St James's Church, the elaborately-carved Norman doorway above you stood unchanged since the 11th century, until it was bombed during the Blitz.

To the left, scarred earth left by the recently-demolished swimming pool fringes the main road and, across the street, stand the flinty bastions of the generic St James's Shopping Centre. To the right, however, one can still imagine oneself at the epicentre of ancient Dover. Tucked into the chalk under Castle Hill Road, the White Horse has stood since the 1360s. Originally the St James's verger's house, it has been an ale house since 1574.

The cellar was once used as a morgue for those drowned at sea but, more positively, since the early 2000s Channel swimmers have signed their names and times on the walls of the bar, creating what appears to be a folk-art tattoo of names from all over the world. The walls are now full, according to the current landlords but, with good English beer and pub food, the White Horse — Dover's oldest pub — carries on eating, drinking and being merry, the ruins of St James's next door reminding us of the transience of all things.

Photograph: Mary Glow

EVERYWHERE MEANS SOMETHING TO SOMEONE

FORT BURGOYNE

At one time, Dover was worried that the French might attack from the direction of Sandwich. In response, a Palmerston Fort was built on the orders of General Sir John Burgoyne in the 1860s, hidden away behind Dover Castle. The French didn't come.

Never used in anger, Fort Burgoyne (originally named Castle Hill Fort) with its large parade ground, became an area for peacetime military activities. In the late Victorian period, when war was still perceived as glamorous, civilians in uniform would arrive in Dover and march up to the fort to take part in military pageants and re-enactments, much like a few do today at the opposing fortification, the Drop Redoubt.

Fort Burgoyne has a peaceful air of idleness and military lassitude about it: soldiers' graffiti appears everywhere and, in one empty, vaulted casement, a crudely-painted Mickey Mouse and Donald Duck decorate the walls, evidence that the rooms were once used as a day nursery for the nearby Connaught barracks. A previous commander had a goat and an allotment, and a protected colony of bats inhabits one of the many tunnels. Wardens currently protect and maintain the flora and fauna for The Land Trust, which owns the scheduled ancient monument, while they examine its future potential.

Photograph: Rebecca Sperini

EVERYWHERE MEANS SOMETHING TO SOMEONE

The idea of the Greeters came from Lyn Brooks in Brooklyn, New York. Lyn was heartbroken that her friends didn't feel safe enough to walk around New York on their own. So, she organised a few tour guides of local people to take them round Brooklyn, and that grew and grew and became the Big Apple Greeters. The Dover Greeters were set up next with the help of Lyn because of the London Olympics. They started the Calais Greeters, and the Dover Greeters twinned with them so folk coming to and from the Olympics could see local towns. There are so many international Greeters now: Paris, Tokyo, Sydney, Vienna, I think there are 126 destinations now! It's just incredible, it's all run by volunteers happily taking you for a free walk in their hometown.

Photograph: Dover Greeters

EVERYWHERE MEANS SOMETHING TO SOMEONE

Dover should be known for this chap here: Charles Stewart Rolls. He made history here. He was the first person to fly across the Channel in both directions without landing. He and his partner, Henry Royce, who lived in Dover for some time, were also the ones who invented the Rolls Royce car and the Rolls Royce aero engine, the best engines in the world.

Photograph: Rebecca Sperini

The area where you'll find the police station and fire station is called Ladywell after The Well of Our Lady, the town's first drinking fountain, which was installed with a pump in 1834. The sick and the lame congregated here, as it was claimed the water cured all kinds of sickness.

....

Ladywell owes its name to the original source of the water used by the brethren of the Maison Dieu Hospital, which was included within the building's grounds close to the Lady Chapel. The water from the well was said to be 'of a chalybeate character with curative properties', supposedly able to 'work many miracles' and cure many forms of sickness. Following the Reformation, the well was built into '...a nook in the Maison Dieu wall, with two or three steps for people to go down and dip their water vessels.' When Dover Corporation purchased the Maison Dieu, the well was covered, and a pump installed with a ladle attached later for the benefit of wayfarers. In 1866 the splendidly-named Alexander Bottle analysed the water and declared that '...the long celebrated Ladywell water' was 'not fit for human consumption'. The pump was removed and the well finally closed over in 1883.

Photograph: Rebecca Sperini

On both sides of the Channel there were Bronze Age and Stone Age settlements which had artefacts in common. They call it a meritocracy, where there are communities across the sea, and they're connected and trading.

The Bronze Age boat is just amazing, and the big trees that they made the boat from... apparently there aren't any trees that size in our area of Europe; the nearest huge trees like that are in Poland, because in our part of Europe they've been cut down and used for centuries, which doesn't allow them to grow so large. They used yew withies, which were made pliable, to stitch the boat together, and between the planks they put sphagnum moss, with beeswax to make it waterproof. It's just amazing! I wonder whether they've got the last third of the boat out. Where they've knocked the buildings down, you know where the Banksy was, on the opposite side of the subway... where you come out of the subway to go into town there's buildings opposite each other and if they've knocked them down now, they might have extracted the last third of the boat, as a third of it was still under the buildings.

Photograph: Mary Glow

It's like the Hollywood sign. I almost feel like worshipping the cliff. People always look up when they pass the house. Everyone with their heads right back, taking photos. Loads of tourists and walkers see the cliffs from the top, whereas down here is this mad proximity, with the houses so closely underneath; it makes it look even more theatrical and even more fake. There's something about the angle that's very Powell and Pressburger — *Black Narcissus* — it just looks like it's a made-up thing. It's nature, the *sublime*, which is a cheesy word... it's just like the total indifference and power and beauty, and that it's been there for millions of years. It used to be a seabed. The potency and totemic-ness of it just dwarfs you; you feel like a silly, little human being ant next to its power. It's almost religious.

It's made up of the skeletal remains of tiny little living creatures, planktonic algae which formed a white ooze on the seabed. What you can see in lots of places is the veneer of the cliff, which is lots of concrete and cement to stop it from falling down; when you get closer it looks so white, and is covered in net.

Photograph: Loz Chalk

EVERYWHERE MEANS SOMETHING TO SOMEONE

Welcome to the
Ferry Terminal

PORT OF
DOVER

We have a ghost at my house. He's funny. He doesn't hate my dad, but he likes to play jokes on my dad, throwing stuff at him. Closing doors behind him.

Our house is falling apart, it's on Victoria Street. It was a train station during the Second World War, and we think that the ghost, who we call Robert, was actually an Air Force pilot. We researched who used to live in the house, and there was this Air Force pilot who lived in the house called Robert something.

It's really cool. He throws stuff, he closes doors, it's not angry though. We moved in on the 31st March, 15 years ago. I was a baby, and I've lived with him my whole life. The very first thing he did when we moved in, which I think was closing the washing machine door, we all just said, "Robert!" and that name just stuck. It was years later when we researched the house and discovered that a Robert lived there, which is so weird.

He's part of the family. To think we're having to move out because of the landlord, and we have to leave Robert. It's really sad to leave him behind.

There's also a bunker underneath my garden.

Photograph: Susan Pilcher

Archcliffe was a military fort. The walls are 15 feet thick, so if a shell hit it could take the damage. The idea was they needed to stay in this fort with the rest of everything going on, and not be moved out or destroyed by the enemy. It was called a sea fort; there are sea forts all along the cliffs. The Western Heights is covered in the remains of forts, bunkers, gun emplacements — it's really covered. The military let it go derelict in the 80s, but Emmaus is here now, and people pop in all the time.

There's a booklet in the Emmaus shop that shows the original layout of the fort. It was called Archcliffe Military Fort, but a lot was demolished to make way for the new road. It has been an occupied site for so long, when they were doing some digging, I found some Roman coins and brooches. There used to be a big covered tunnel with guns on that hill which went right down to the seashore.

Photograph: Strange Cargo

EVERYWHERE MEANS SOMETHING TO SOMEONE

FISHMONGER'S LANE

Fishmonger's Lane, near the Market Square, led to Fishmonger's Gate, where fishermen used to wash their nets in the river flowing there. A small fishmarket traded here in around 1831. Today the lane provides access from the town centre to St James's shopping and commercial estate.

Flying Horse Lane, next to Fishmonger's Lane, is named after the Flying Horse Inn from where coaches departed daily for Deal and to London.

....

I went to the nearby infant and then primary school, St Mary's in Queen Street, just off Fishmonger's Lane, and lived very close by. Queen Street was demolished to make way for the new A20. So, every day I walked past this pub and at lunchtimes, as I went home to dinner, I went next door to the sweet shop called Fox's to buy sweets for other children in my class. They would give me their pennies and a list of what they would like, and I would take them back after lunch.

Photograph: Strange Cargo

EVERYWHERE MEANS SOMETHING TO SOMEONE

My dad was born in Syros in Greece; his dad was the manager of the Eastern Telegraph Company, an English company laying cables around the world, and Syros was a major centre for the whole of the Mediterranean for pulling cables. The nearest school to Syros that they could find in England was Dover College, so my dad's journey to school involved getting a ferry from Syros to Athens, another ferry from Athens to Marseille, a train from Marseille to Paris, where he was met by a representative from Thomas Cook, and then a train to Calais and a ferry to Dover, where he went to school. He could only go home once a year, and his own mother didn't even recognise him when she visited, as he'd grown so much.

One of the things that Dad used to tell me about Dover was that once a year all the Dover College boys would swim across the harbour. Eventually he got a scholarship to Oxford — he was very bright, my dad — and the College gave the whole school the day off, as it was the first time a Dover College boy had been awarded a scholarship to Oxford.

Photograph: Susan Pilcher

EVERYWHERE MEANS SOMETHING TO SOMEONE

Many of the streets on Buckland Estate, built between 1946 and 1950, carry American and Canadian names. Hundreds of early homes were imported, prefabricated houses manufactured in USA and Canada. The prefabs housed many families whose Dover homes were destroyed by enemy action. Post-war German prisoners of war helped to dig the trenches that were designed to house the estate's infrastructure.

Photograph: Rebecca Sperini

SIMCOE TERRACE

Flats 2L 3I

Wellesley Road links the seafront and the A2 next to the Gateway flats, and it's named after the Duke of Wellington, whose name was Arthur Wellesley. The Grand Hotel occupied the site in the 1890s, but it was demolished after serious damage by attacking German and Italian aircraft in 1940.

Townwall Street is now part of the busy A20, and it faces the harbour and the Gateway flats. It was named in 1799 after the defensive wall that surrounded the old town. Freemen, at one stage, were responsible for the upkeep of this wall, which was pulled down in 1818. Some salvaged materials from the town wall were reused to build Kearsney Abbey in 1821.

The area of Woolcomber Street was once a saltpan. The street was built on land formed since 1500, but before the houses were built the lower end was made up of areas of saltpans. After the Second World War there were only two houses left standing, although the area has been built upon since 1638. It was here that locals combed sheeps' wool to disentangle and straighten out the fibres to prepare for spinning. According to legend it was from this area that English kings, with their knights, set off from the harbour to go to battle in France.

Photograph: Rebecca Sperini

EVERYWHERE MEANS SOMETHING TO SOMEONE

In a town that was built on seafaring, boats, shipping and sailing vessels, there is one remaining ships' chandler. Sharp and Enright is across from Dover Marina — a stranded sailor can walk across the road for dozens of varieties of yacht varnish, deck paint, fittings, rope and stainless-steel cable, cut to order.

Established 1865 as a sail maker, the traditional painted shop front, acquired in 1925, still resonates that period, its stock displayed in the window for practical rather than decorative purposes. Kettles and hurricane lamps hang alongside gimballed compasses and brass clocks, coils of rope, cleats, and anti-fouling paint. Brightly coloured buoys and inflatable tenders are often tied up in the doorway. You can buy a traditional canvas fisherman's smock; there are seven anchors to choose from. Inside, helpful men in duster coats know every washer and rivet, metric and imperial, watched over by an imposing matriarch, Sarah Sharp, the highly respected and knowledgeable scion of the firm and the fifth generation of the family to run the store.

....

I always get the chains and shackles here. It's an amazing little marine supply shop which has been there as long as I can remember. Established in 1865 originally as a sail maker. I always enjoy my annual trip there.

Photograph: Mary Glow

A Banksy, usually gifted at night and in secret, is a mixed blessing for a town.

Some councils see the unlicensed artwork as a positive boost for civic PR; some feel it presents them with a preservation problem they wish they didn't have; for others it is simply vandalism.

The Dover Banksy, an apparently Brexit-themed piece, appeared overnight in May 2017 on an empty Victorian building which was scheduled for demolition: a highly visible structure near the ferry terminal. Painted a year after the referendum, the Banksy portrayed a worker chipping away one of the stars from the European flag. The Dover Banksy quickly gained national and international coverage — his largest and most prominent work to date. The Banksy created a lively buzz and controversy within Dover, not only about its subject matter, but also its worth — the mural clearly added enormous value to the derelict building, maybe it was more valuable than the building itself?

The debate was swiftly resolved in 2019 as — as quickly as it had arrived — the Banksy was overpainted, overnight. Then, in November 2023, the wall on which it was painted was demolished. As with most of Banksy's work, the discussions around the Dover Banksy are as interesting as the mural itself.

Photograph: Mary Glow

When we were in our early 20s, espresso coffee bars were just opening and there was Elizabeth's in the Market Square; I think it was named after the owner's wife or daughter. It's where KFC stands now, and that's where we met. I had just come back to Dover to teach. We had mutual friends, and one day we all met in Elizabeth's, which became a frequent thing.

It was the 1960s, and my mother didn't disapprove of coffee shops — she didn't think I should go to pubs, and in fact I didn't until I went in with my boyfriend, now husband. Some other mothers didn't even approve of coffee shops. That's where young people met: coffee bars were a new thing, cafés were where ladies would have afternoon tea or coffee, but coffee bars catered for the general population really, including young people, they were respectable and there hadn't been an equivalent. The machines used to make a hissing, bubbling noise when they made the espresso; it was frothy coffee.

Photograph: Rebecca Sperini

EVERYWHERE MEANS SOMETHING TO SOMEONE

It was run by two sisters, one was a widow and one was unmarried; I forget their names. The pubs then were so different in the 1960s — you had the jug and bottle section, it's still there except they've knocked the division down. There used to be a door where you'd go into the jug and bottle and they used to serve you a jug of beer, or a bottle of beer, then you'd have the saloon bar and the public bar. You wouldn't take your girlfriend to the public bar.

Photograph: Mary Glow

EVERYWHERE MEANS SOMETHING TO SOMEONE

In the middle of the road in front of the old St James's Church, before they hit demolition mode, there was a *pissoir* — a French style public urinal. It was a small cylindrical building with a domed roof. I remember using it after the war and there were shrapnel holes in it, which people use to peep out of. I always wondered if someone got caught in the act when the shells came down. The pissoir was demolished and ended up in storage at Connaught Park. I wonder if its still there somewhere?

Photograph: Rebecca Sperini

There are only two places in this country, as I understand it, that have French names. We are one, the other is London; Londres and Douvres, so that distinguishes us.

Douvres probably comes from the Celtic *dubras*, meaning waters. Further south in France and in northern Italy, there are many Dovers of various spellings; these may derive from the *dubris* or the Gaulish *dubron*, again meaning waters.

Photograph: Susan Pilcher

Ray Warner started Dover Film Festival in 1947. He'd been in war reconnaissance, and he opened a photography shop in Townwall Street.

They had an exhibition on at the Beacon that they're building over on Bench Street. The architect asked us on what we thought and I said, "You do realise the frontage on Townwall Street was where Ray Warner had his photographic shop?" He said, "Who is Ray Warner"? I said, "Well, he started the Dover Film Festival and Dover has a unique record going back right from 1947 to this current year."

Ray died in 1990, and Phil Heath took over for ten years, but when he stopped no one picked it up. I thought, I can't let this unique record lapse, so I arranged showing my first Dover film in the council chambers.

I had some footage that made up the films for 2000 and 2001. I showed it in 2003, as the Chairman of Dover District Council invited guests. We were able to use all the seats in the Council Chamber. The Dover film is now shown annually in the first week in March at the Silver Screen.

Photograph: Susan Pilcher

ANNUAL DOVER FILM

Showing at the Cinema in the Dover Museum

3rd - 9th March 2024
www.dover-film.com

1983 DOVER FILM by Ray Warner will be shown after the 2023 Dover Film.

The run time for both films is 45 minutes.

The Dover Film is a collection of the key events in our local community.

TELEPHONE : 07704 930892 for further details

Seats can be reserved in person at the Dover Visitor Information Centre in the Market Square, Dover.

BOOK ahead to avoid disappointment

Ray Warner

Images below from 1983 Dover Film.

Images below from 2023 Dover Film.

My grandmother, Susan Gatehouse, was born at the bottom of Shakespeare Cliff. They were a fishing family there, and they lived in one of the few little houses below the cliff. The only way to get into Dover was to sail round or climb up the cliff to go to Hougham. I did hear that there were twins born there and the doctor stopped the train so he could get off in the middle of the track to attend their birth.

Photograph: Rebecca Sperini

My father, Douglas Richards, was an engineer at Solex in London. At night during the Blitz, he was a gun position commander at the Battersea two inch rocket battery. During the day he made engine parts and precision instruments. Solex also had a special projects office, run by a senior engineer, which solved War Office problem cases. Among other things, it fixed six pounder recoil slides and detonation circuit timers. When V1 buzz bombs started, there was a project to mechanically slave batteries of 3.7 inch AA guns to a radar director. There is a 3.7″ AA gun at Dover Castle near the main gate. My father, being well qualified by then, was the man sent to install these, along all the fixed routes that they flew along, until the Germans developed mobile launch ramps. While they had fixed launch ramps, the V1 paths were very predictable and these batteries had a near 100% success rate, helped by the new VT fuse proximity detonation. Before these advances, it was estimated you needed 20,000 shells to destroy an aircraft. The US Navy said the VT fuse was the biggest leap forward and the closest guarded secret of the Second World War. It saved countless lives from kamikaze later in 1944.

Photograph: Rebecca Sperini

It was interesting to read in the *Mercury* about the windmills that used to exist around Dover. One mill remaining in almost intact condition is Ripple Mill, clearly visible on the Dover to Deal road. My great grandfather John Banks lived and worked at Ripple Mill from 1881 to the early part of the last century. His daughter, my grandmother, Julie Annette Banks was killed by a shell which landed on Dover Priory station in September 1944. She'd married my grandfather Charles Henry Green in 1906, and my father Charles John Green was born in 1908.

I presume that the mill was, like a lot of property around East Kent, part of the Kitchener family estate, as sometime before the First World War my father was playing in the mill yard when the great General himself came to pay a visit. The most iconic and memorable image people have of Lord Kitchener is of his patriotic outstretched arm and the caption 'Your Country Needs You!' My father's image of Lord Kitchener was of a moustachioed hero in full uniform rushing around the mill yard towing my dad's toy wooden train on the end of a piece of string to keep the children amused.

Photograph: Mary Glow

We laid wreaths at the Zeebrugge Raid cemetery. As a First World War memorial, there were lots of bravery awards. It turned the tide of the war in Belgium, so all the Belgians came over for the awards. It happens to coincide with St George's Day on 23rd April.

The Zeebrugge Raid was an attempt by the Royal Navy to block the Belgian port of Bruges-Zeebrugge. The British intended to sink obsolete ships in the canal entrance, to prevent German vessels from leaving port. The raid began with a diversion against the mile-long Zeebrugge mole, which provided shelter for U-boats in the harbour and protected access to their inland base. The attack was led by the old cruiser *Vindictive* with two Mersey ferries, *Daffodil* and *Iris II*. The three ships were accompanied by two old submarines, which were filled with explosives to blow up the viaduct connecting the mole to the shore. By 12:05am on 23rd April 1918, the port was successfully blocked.

The *Vindictive's* flag is inside the Dover Town Council building. The Mayor always rings the Zeebrugge Bell at noon from the Town Hall balcony to mark the day.

Photograph: Amy West

EVERYWHERE MEANS SOMETHING TO SOMEONE

As 13-year-olds, my friend Susan and I used to visit her mum. Her mother used to run the W H Smith store, you know, the newspaper store in Marine Station. In its day it was a really amazing place, a beautiful building, and the trains used to come in like the Pullman — so grand. They were cross-Channel passengers, so, on a Sunday morning, Sue and I used to take a trolley of papers across the platforms to the Pullman train when it came in. Every time I go there, the smell, everything about that reminds me of being 13. The carriages had little lights and the seats were all cream and brown. Carl was one of the stewards on the Pullman, he'd be on from London — I must remember to ask Sue if she remembers Carl.

Photograph: Strange Cargo

EVERYWHERE MEANS SOMETHING TO SOMEONE

My dear old mum had a beautiful, long-cased grandfather clock that stood in my grandparents' house. She left it to me. I wasn't in Dover at the time, so I offered it to Dover Museum, who were delighted. There were two conditions: it must stay on permanent display, and it must stay on the time it stopped — don't adjust the dial. It has a hand-painted Chinese style face, a pagoda with Mandarin and Chinese flowers, probably done to somebody's order. I believe the clock maker's daughter did it; it was amateur, but delightful in its own way. The clockmaker was David Steber. His father John had been a Bavarian clock maker specialising in rifle mechanisms, and had come to Dover in a garrison. John had ten children and a shop in Cannon Street. He died in 1819 and his son took over the business, selling watches, clocks, jewellery, and fancy haberdashery. We know this from an inventory from 1834 when he filed as bankrupt and fled to New York. David moved around, marrying twice more, and he opened a watch and clock maker's shop. Unfortunately, the maker of the clock that sits in the Crundall Room in Dover Museum drowned in the Tuscaloosa river in 1869.

Photograph: Amy West

EVERYWHERE MEANS SOMETHING TO SOMEONE

BY VRONNIE WARD

Wind on the White Cliffs whistling a bygone age,
Trees bend to its power like an aging stoop,
Over the chalk, welcoming and repelling in equal measure,
Paths wind their spaghetti across the emerald green.

Skylarks singing their melodious tunes amongst the sea grass,
Sun on skin, inhale the sea air, its salty twang,
The ferry port clangs and hoots its business ongoing day and night,
Boats sail back and forth spewing their inanimate or human cargo.

Godsend cliffs in times of crisis beckons us still,
No war, invasion or virus can shatter this mighty chalk,
A chance to think, walk, dream or die,
Of bravery against all the odds.

Fortress stone standing strong, majestic and true,
Tunnels hold their secrets close... khaki, blue and navy,
The throbbing heartbeat of Spitfire, Hurricane,
We'll meet again.

Photograph: Rebecca Sperini

Lorna Bomford lived in Milestone House in Temple Ewell for a number of years until her death in 1962. A suffragette, she was also one of Dover's first female councillors, an accomplished artist, and she served as a Justice of the Peace.

Photograph: Rebecca Sperini

EVERYWHERE MEANS SOMETHING TO SOMEONE

Flint is a very odd material. I don't pretend to understand the chemical process in which the remains of silicate sponges separated out into a strata of lumpy nodules in the calcite deposits at the bottom of a shallow sea, but they did, and here they are — black and grey, hard, brittle, shining and incorruptible. It is the fieldstone of downland Kent. No doubt it was piled up in loose walls to enclose stock or mark boundaries, but the Romans brought mortar with them, and more ambitious structures arose, like the Pharos and the succession of forts which underlie the heart of Dover.

Those walls fell and new walls were built with the same flints: town walls, churches. More flints were carted in, and the town grew, walls falling and rising — hospitals, schools, mills, tanneries, breweries and houses. Their faces might be brick or dressed stone, but at the back are the same flints, used and reused. So, look around your town, anywhere, everywhere. Any flint in any wall could have been part of a Roman castle, a Saxon priory, a medieval leper hospital — or it could have been bought at £500 a ton from a builders' merchant last year.

Photograph: Amy West

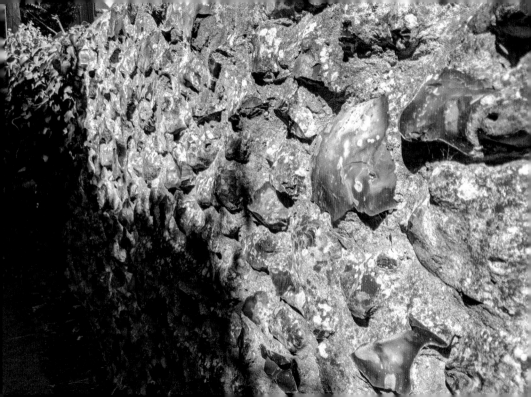

My boyfriend, later my husband, used to ride his motorbike to the Top Hat in Dover. It was a 60s coffee bar — it had an upstairs, and it was a magnet for cool people. They served coffee, tea, cake, stuff like that. I think it's where Aspendos is now. We all wore jeans and leather jackets, as it was a real biker destination. I still remember my boyfriend's bike: it was a Triumph 500, registration number GFN 881. They had a juke box which was tuppence a play, or sixpence for three songs. Motown was a favourite, and Tom Jones. I'm a bit of an Elvis fan myself, and had an Elvis impersonator for my 80th birthday. It was an evening destination for us, although it probably opened in the day too when we were at work. It was a big meeting place for teenagers. You'd buy a cake and sit there all night, put money in the jukebox for a bit of music. Then I'd hop on a double decker at 1am and head home to Aycliffe on the last bus.

The mods and rockers were always outside with motorbikes and scooters. There was often a little argy-bargy, but nothing too violent. It was just how it was.

Photograph: Strange Cargo

I was born in Tower Street and went to Sunday school there, and we used to go with Sister Bessie from the Wesleyan Mission Hall to the caves where the chalk pits are, by the steps that go up to the station; the chalk was used in the local lime making businesses.

....

The op-art painting on the front of the old Mission Hall was painted by Dover artist Simon Bill, and was part of a project organised by Dover Arts Development (DAD).

Photograph: Mary Glow

My brother John and I would visit the Victoria Hospital in our St John's uniforms as teenagers in the evening to help feed the elderly patients. It's a block of flats now, but it is a beautiful building. That's how my nursing career started. I had my appendix out when I was 11 and my dad had his hernia fixed there too. Children couldn't visit, so we used to go down the lane at the side of the hospital and wave to him at the window. I retired in 1996, but I worked in Buckland Hospital on the surgical ward until then.

Photograph: Rebecca Sperini

I don't know where else I could live after this: the port, the drama, the nature. We hear owls and birds and rats and foxes, it's such a dramatic environment. There were protests only a couple of days ago — the tractors were protesting. You hear the horns and all that noise; the sonicness of the port. You become used to it, and it becomes part of your ambience. A few weeks ago, everything went silent for just a short time, and I've never heard that before, as the rest of the time there's a constant rumble and the windows shake; the seagulls, the cars, the trucks.

When we came to see this house, I thought it was amazing and so close to the sea; we got married on the beach over the road. Dover still has a reputation, and it can be really abrasive sometimes, but it always surprises me that the people here are absolutely amazing. I often think that people are going to assume things about me, but people here are just really, very free and every time I have a conversation with someone, they surprise me. And that's a pretty strong thing to be able to say, that people surprise you.

Photograph: Strange Cargo

EVERYWHERE MEANS SOMETHING TO SOMEONE

During the War we lived in Widred Road. My mum had made me some trousers to wear in the Anderson shelter out of the itchiest blanket fabric, and she told me that I had to wear them. I'd always cry when I had to put them on but would always fall asleep in them in the shelter. Anderson shelters were supplied to people to put in their gardens to protect us from bomb attacks during wartime. After the war my dad took it out and turned it into a cycle store.

There were several companies that produced Anderson shelters during wartime, but of the 3.6 million shelters built, just a handful remain in place today. Many of them have the initials H O painted on the inside, which indicates they were made by a Home Office-approved manufacturer.

Photograph: Strange Cargo

It was all open fields and Army buildings across there. On YouTube there's a film of Dover in 1947, of the prefabs being built, as there was a major housing shortage after the war because we'd been so heavily bombed here.

The prefabs were so cold, and there was always black mould. I lived in one of them from aged two to 12; they were called American prefabs. The Americans were so fond of Dover after the Second World War, they donated money to the town for a hospital. Canadians were stationed here during the war too. Some of the street names give us a clue — Colorado Close, Washington Way. We lived in Monks Way in the English prefabs — Abbots Walk, Friars Way, all names connected to the Canterbury Pilgrim's Way. The donkeys at Margate seafront overwintered in the fields behind our house and we had free rides all winter.

Photograph: Mary Glow

MAINE CLOSE

One day I was working here as a volunteer, and Paul Jarvis and Tony Staveley said, "How do you fancy being a tour guide, Alan?" and I said, "Not really." They kept on at me for three or four weeks, so I had to give in. They trained me up to be a tour guide and I passed first time. Then, about six weeks later, Paul said, "Are you in on a Wednesday, Alan?" The next Wednesday we had 75 children come in and we had to do half in the morning, half in the afternoon, and that was my first tour. About four weeks later, Paul and Tony used to come in on a Sunday and I was here, all nice and quiet, and then Paul said, "Do you fancy being a miller?" and I said, "Nah", but I had to give in. They trained me up and I passed first time on that. We lost Paul ten years ago now and we've lost Tony now too, and now I'm the Head Miller and that's why I have my license up on the wall. I have a young lad who's trained up. The Mill is open 9am till 3pm and I get through about a ton of grain a year.

Photograph: Amy West

Many years ago, my late grandfather used to work at the Western Docks before the days of the roll-on, roll-off ferries. Back then, cars were loaded onto a pallet and craned on. For safety reasons, the cars weren't allowed to have any fuel in their tanks, so my grandad's job was to drain the petrol tanks. He'd then sell it back to someone else at a profit. Very entrepreneurial!

Photograph: Strange Cargo

BROOKFIELD AVENUE

My husband had an uncle with a general store, where Dover Glass Centre is now. They sold everything: bacon, next to cycle repair kits, next to ladies' tights. The shop was owned by Eddie Partridge, who had a special affinity with animals — he was a bit of a Dr Doolittle, and Auntie Binney was his wife. Michael Bentine, who was one of the Goons, was even known to have talked about Eddie Partridge and his shop on the radio one day.

It was at the bottom of Green Lane, in the Brookfield Road area. You can look it up in Kelly's Directory. The shop was there for years, it was one of those corner shops that were there forever. Eddie came down here during wartime and they lived in Shepherdswell and had a tennis court in their garden.

Photograph: Mary Glow

EVERYWHERE MEANS SOMETHING TO SOMEONE

Visiting Dover Castle as a boy, I was fascinated to watch a member of staff light an oil-soaked rag and drop it down the well. Seeing it go down such a long way for ages was amazing — down, down, down, it seemed it would never land at the bottom. I know that people used to drop a coin down too, and count how many seconds it took before you could hear it bounce.

....

I went on a primary school trip. It was when Henry VIII's huge suit of armour was still on display in the main hall. We walked all around, saw the breathtaking views from the ramparts, peered through arrow slits, marvelled at the thickness of the walls and read panels telling us about its long history. We made our way down to explore the labyrinth of tunnels and cold, stone-grey rooms below the Castle, which is where the thing I remember most about the trip revealed itself. As we ran down a set of spiral steps into a dimly lit room, there, right in the middle of the floor was the biggest poo I have ever seen in my life! Unfortunately, that poo still looms large in my memory of Dover Castle.

Photograph: Amy West

I live in Queens Avenue which leads onto the Whinless Down nature reserve, which is really beautiful. The bluebell woods in spring at Elms Vale Park are so lovely, and the Connaught Park ponies are up there on and off too, and they have the Angus cattle with long horns. Lots of people do their doggie walking up there, and the view at the top... you can see right over to the docks and Dover Castle and Coombe Valley. It's wonderful year-round if you have your wellingtons and are dressed right. There's football in the season on the field and there's Astor and Archers Court schools — which is now called White Cliffs Academy — they use it for cross-country running. The wildlife with woodpeckers, all sorts of birds, foxes. The wildlife is phenomenal up there. Sometimes you see the children from Harbour school doing their nature walks.

Photograph: Mary Glow

OLD MATERNITY HOSPITAL, VICTORIA CRESCENT

/// YEARS.LIMES.FROCK

I was born in 1948 in the hospital opposite Victoria Crescent. It was the maternity hospital back then, and lots of Dover babies were born there. My brother was born there too. Buckland Hospital was a lovely hospital, but it was knocked down some years back and a new one built on the site. They saved my daughter's life there when she was three years old; she was rushed into hospital and had peritonitis, you know, a ruptured appendix. She was three weeks in hospital.

Photograph: Strange Cargo

INSTITUTED AT THE GENERAL THANKSGIVING OF MDCCCXLIX

My dad was a tank driver, and when he left the Army we moved to Dover, because my mum was a Dovorian.

When I married my husband — Dover born and bred — I moved to Westbury Road where I've been 37 years in April. In my street, we don't have any problems. I like the people around me. They call me the Westbury Rottie because I keep an eye on everyone, and don't take any crap. We have a good sense of community. I keep Calpol in my house and the mums come over whenever they're in need with the kids. I help out in the community. It's a true neighbourhood. The kids all know, if there's any trouble whatsoever, they all come and bang on my door.

It's a long cul-de-sac, and more or less everyone knows each other. The new ones that move in get to know people. Now we have our own community centre on the hill, on Belgrave Hill, called the Clarendon and Westbury Community Association. There's a warm hub, feed the family, and a youth club. I used to help run the youth club.

Photograph: Rebecca Sperini

We went to Dover Castle, running around the ramparts with my brother. We went up one of the steep embankments, where you're probably not meant to be; I remember there was a big gun or something up there. Well, I ran back down and over the edge of this rampart, and fell a few feet onto my head and was knocked completely static. I think my brother went off and got my mum and dad, as I was just rolling around on the floor moaning, and when they got back there were a few people gathered around me.

There was a woman that I kind of vaguely remember as I was coming round, and she was pressing a coin onto my head, and I never knew why someone would do that, but she was pressing this, what was the biggest coin she had, probably an old 50p, saying, "This will keep the swelling down." Anyway, they got her away from me, but I was completely out of it. She didn't know the first thing about first aid, and that ended our day out at Dover Castle.

Photograph: Susan Pilcher

In 1969 Father Bill Sheargold retired to Dover and set up Dover's 69 Motorcycle Club. Originally using the old military stables on the cliffs as their club house, they hosted two annual rallies. The White Cliffs Rally became a must-attend venue for bikers from all around the world, and many thousands used to descend on Dover for the weekend of the event; on the Sunday morning of the rally the bikers all used to head into Dover to attend a church service at St Nicholas given by Father Bill. The last, I remember, had a Triumph Hurricane and a 1200 Harley Davidson on the altar. The noise of all the bikes being kicked into life at the same time was just thunderously wonderful, and I will treasure the memory for all time.

....

I started going when I was 16, as I dated a biker. But it's important to us as older bikers to engage younger people, to show them that it's a cheap way of getting about, but you've got to be safe. So, we take the bikes to carparks, and people like to coo over a nice bike, and it gives us a chance to talk to them. 69 Club bikers love raising money for charity; we go out, we ride, we eat cake, we raise money.

Photograph: Mary Glow

Dieu Stone Lane links the main street at St Mary's Church and Maison Dieu Road. It is so named from the time that this area, which is next to Pencester Gardens, was marshy, so stones were put down to help monks walking from Dover Castle to St Mary's Church.

Photograph: Mary Glow

I used to cycle daily to my job at Hatton's. My husband's sister shouted to me one day as I was cycling to work, "Barbara, Rory wants to take you out!" He took me to the beach front and, in time, we got married.

It was freezing in Hatton's. The floor was solid concrete, and I got chilblains all over my feet. At lunch we used to go up to the old living quarters to warm up. We even used to warm up our sandwiches on the electric fires, how we never started a fire!

....

My surname's Hatton, like the shop! I used to work there as a girl too. Upstairs were living quarters where old staff used to live, they didn't live there when I worked there, but the quarters remained. It's where W H Smith's is now, if you look up to the top you can see 'Hatton' in the stone, right at the very top.

Photograph: Mary Glow

My friend Gerald used to make soap box carts. They were made of wood and we'd find some wheels, any wheels — we'd get them from peoples gardens, we would *usually* ask. We'd then race them down the hill from Mount Road to Manor Road.

My mum and grandma were the first to have a fridge on Manor Road. I remember people coming round for ice cubes and my mum hiding because we wouldn't have any made. I would tell her to just make more, and she could tell them to come back.

Photograph: Mary Glow

There was a Dr Who story called *The Mind of Evil,* originally aired on BBC1 between Saturday 30th January and Saturday 6th March 1971, which was all about how they were trying to rehabilitate violent prisoners by using a thing called the Keller machine, which projected the prisoners' worst fears, and this was supposedly meant to rehabilitate them to become less violent, but (obviously, as it was Dr Who) the Keller machine had an alien parasite inside, and the Master, who was played by Roger Delgado, was behind it.

It was all done at a prison called Stangmore, and Dover Castle was the location that was used for the prison. There was a big shoot-out between the Unit soldiers, you know the Unit with the Brigadier and all that sort of thing, and they had a prison riot there and a big shoot-out between the Unit soldiers and the prisoners, in the grounds of Dover Castle. It was an early Jon Pertwee episode, in his second series. You see them coming up towards the drawbridge in Bessy, the yellow car, and the riot inside the Castle keep.

Photograph: Mary Glow

EVERYWHERE MEANS SOMETHING TO SOMEONE

I lived at Aycliffe from the age of two until 1987, when my house blew away in the hurricane. We were the last block at the end of Aycliffe and my dad said, "Oooh, it's sounding a bit rough out there. I think we should get out." The following morning our house was gone, the windows, everything was all broken, my car had reversed into my dad's car, my brother's motorbike was under a pile of roof tiles. But the milkman still delivered the milk, I don't know how that happened, but the milk was there so we could have a cup of tea in the morning. We'd had to wait until the weather calmed down before we went outside, and basically all four houses had gone. We had to live with friends because we had nowhere to go; we were homeless. My dad had been considering buying the house, he had all his cheques and everything, and all his bills, but what happened was the wind broke the back window, blew through the house, went up the stairs, along the passage and all his cheques and bills went out through the roof along with my mother's birthday cards.

Photograph: Strange Cargo

EVERYWHERE MEANS SOMETHING TO SOMEONE

The hovercraft to Calais was fast, it only took 35 minutes, and it was such a novelty. It could take cars and coaches. If the weather got too bad, or it broke down, we sometimes got stranded and came back on the ferry. Then, of course, they introduced the Seacat catamaran. I never worked on that, it came later. The two hovercraft companies, Hoverlloyd in Ramsgate and Seaspeed from Dover, merged. My friend Linda said, "What are they going to call it, *Hoverspeed*?" And they did! Hoverspeed ran until it couldn't get repairs anymore. Originally, they went from Dover Eastern Docks, and then the craft was chopped in half and stretched, and then they went from Western Docks Hoverport. It was advertised as London to Paris or Brussels, and people loved it. I wish I'd kept some of the leaflets.

....

My grandad used to take me to look through the portholes on the pier at the hovercraft coming and going. I can't describe if you've never seen it how impressive those bloody things were, when they rose up and inflated and they shot off down the beach. As a small child, looking through these concrete walls with portholes, it was really quite exhilarating. There is a propeller from one of them preserved at Marine Station at the Western Docks.

Photograph: Strange Cargo

EVERYWHERE MEANS SOMETHING TO SOMEONE

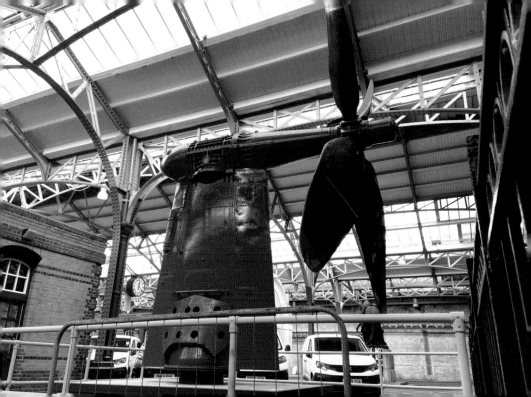

My favourite view was from Mayfield Avenue, my old house was there, and I could look out and see both the sea and the surrounding fields all at the same time. I used to be able to hear all the boats coming and going. Dover is so multi-layered you can see so many different perspectives.

Photograph: Susan Pilcher

Going back to 1825, the miller's youngest boy Edward died on level three in the mill. He was playing in the flour hopper; he was just four years old. Only 18 months before that, his older brother William had died in the cog pit — he got pulled in by the cogs, he was the age of 14. One of William's jobs was to check the cogs were in properly first thing, but one day he came in late, and his father opened the sluice gate and started the wheel. He heard a scream, but it was too late. So, the miller lost two sons in 18 months. Sometimes I've seen a boy playing on level three, and I get a cold shudder.

Photograph: Amy West

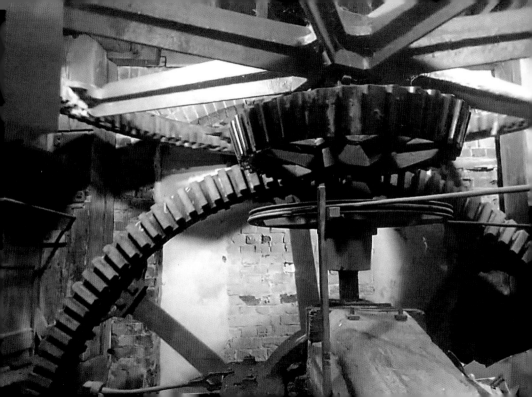

It was a big event to go to visit our grandparents at the Prince Albert pub when we were kids to watch the Dover Carnival. It was a great experience to have a bird's eye view from the upstairs windows with a pile of old pennies on the window sill. The money collectors would hold a sort of purse up to us on a long bamboo pole.

It was here that I first saw decimal coins. They arrived in a tube shape, wrapped in brown paper. My grandparents unwrapped them and gave all the grandchildren one of each denomination.

I have fond memories of visiting in the school holidays, waking up to the sound of seagulls. Grandma used to walk us from there up to the Castle and Grandad would take us out and leave us in the children's room with a coke and a packet of crisps in a number of the local pubs.

Photograph: Strange Cargo

There are big old concrete stones in the ground, which we call Pepper Stones. J W Pepper was Mayor of Dover in 18-something, and he had stones put all around the boundary of Dover with his name on them. The easiest one to see is up on the road from Dover to Deal, up past the Castle with the coach parking on your left had side — right in the far corner of the coach park is a Pepper Stone.

Photograph: Amy West

EVERYWHERE MEANS SOMETHING TO SOMEONE

KEARSNEY ABBEY

Kearsney Abbey is important because if you didn't go to the beach, people would go and play there. You know, Kearsney Abbey is a prime example of a former industrial place that people aren't aware has this whole hidden history.

10,000 years ago, by the end of the last Ice Age, the river Dour flowed through the old mill pond area and a shallow, spring-fed pool developed. In 1689 there was a working mill there that provided income for local people. The River Paper Mill had been a corn mill previously; there were mills all along the river Dour. When you wander through the beautiful Art and Crafts landscaped parkland and see all the brick ruins, most visitors don't know they were part of what had been the watercourse for the mills.

Photograph: Strange Cargo

EVERYWHERE MEANS SOMETHING TO SOMEONE

Dover Engineering Works was famous all over the world for making drain covers. They were called Elkington Gatic, which was stamped on all their drain covers; they were branded as covers for all purposes. The river used to go through their engineering works as part of the cooling process. It's where Morrison's stands now. Opposite used to be the Post Office, the sorting office, that's been taken down now and replaced by housing, which I believe is called Elkington House.

Photograph: Mary Glow

"What in God's name has someone done to that?" an older gentleman said to me, pointing at the doodles on the building.

"I think it's called Art?" I replied.

"Whoever did that should be bloody arrested," said the older man.

"I did it sir," I replied, smiling.

"Oh… well… I feel a bit silly now," said the older gentleman.

"It's okay," I said, "Art's not for everyone."

Photograph: Amy West

EVERYWHERE MEANS SOMETHING TO SOMEONE

The trains would come into Dover Western Docks for the ferry, so you would alight there and catch a ferry to France. Some trains, of course, would go onto the ferries — not the engine, just the carriages. They would be loaded onto the boat, a flat-bottomed boat. There were three of them, the *Twickenham*, the *Hampton*, and the *Shepperton* ferry. The ferry would come into a lock which would fill with water to raise it up to the railway track, and then it would be locked in place so it couldn't move. The train would turn around on a turntable outside and push the carriages onto the boat. People would be asleep in the carriages, because it would be the Orient Express sleeper. Then they would come off the other side and away it went to Paris. The tracks are filled in now, and it's part of the cruise terminal.

Photograph: Mary Glow

You still get bathers in Dover, but not like you used to. Of course, back in those days the beach was where you would have gone for the day, people don't do that now, people go elsewhere. Back then you wouldn't have had the means of going anywhere else. We didn't have a car until I was 11 years old and then, when we did, we'd only use it on Sundays. Dad wouldn't use it to go to work or anything, as we couldn't afford the fuel.

Photograph: Susan Pilcher

JEWISH CEMETERY, OLD CHARLTON ROAD

/// GROW.LOOSE.MERCY

The Jewish cemetery was established in the 1860s on land provided by the Dover Harbour Board. Inside, plaques can be seen on the right-hand wall which were taken from the synagogue that once stood at the seafront before it was demolished. The plaques were there to celebrate some of the synagogue's benefactors. It's through the efforts of the Reverend R I Cohen that the synagogue on Snargate Street came to be, and the biggest of the plaques is there to celebrate him. The burials start at the top of the hill in the top left-hand corner and descend down to the most recent burial of Philip Karl Franks in 1995. At the bottom of the slope, under one of the large mature trees is a beautiful chest tomb where lies the second wife of Rev R I Cohen in pride of place.

Photograph: Amy West

A sailor popped into my tattoo shop a little while back. He was from Scotland and had sailed down from Edinburgh to Dover to work on the tugboats.

He already had quite a few tattoos and was interested in getting more in my style, which is quite traditional. At the time of our appointment, he was technically on duty, so had to ask his ship's captain for permission. We got the go ahead and started tattooing a swallow on his hand.

For sailors, tattoos have historically served as records of important experiences. It's said that sailors once tattooed a swallow on the left side of their chest for travelling 5,000 nautical miles, and another on the right for travelling 10,000 nautical miles. Many others would get the barn swallow tattooed, for its symbolism as a bird that migrates far from home and comes back again.

I was halfway through tattooing the guy when his phone rang: the ship's captain needed him back on a job. I wrapped his hand up and he left, and he came back an hour later and we finished off the tattoo. Tattooing a sailor's swallow, on a sailor, whilst he was away from home, felt like the ultimate sailor story.

Photograph: Rebecca Sperini

EVERYWHERE MEANS SOMETHING TO SOMEONE

Domenico Brilli had all the seafront kiosks; he ran all the ice cream kiosks. He started out, so my grandparents told me, just by selling what they used to call hokey-pokey ice cream from a cart; that was Brilli. He was one of the first Kent Italian ice cream men, and there are still people around with that name. He is buried at St James's Cemetery.

Photograph: Strange Cargo

The tram was overloaded. Apparently he was an inexperienced driver on that route, and he went down the hill too fast. Of course, when the tram came to the corner it toppled over at the bottom and smashed into the wall. Trams were open-topped then, so the passengers were just flung out. The dead were taken to the nearby Cricketers public house, and the injured moved into nearby houses. The most severely injured were taken to the Royal Victoria Hospital on Dover High Street.

The tram accident remains one of the worst on record, and the Dover Society has put up a plaque to commemorate those that died.

Photograph: Amy West

EVERYWHERE MEANS SOMETHING TO SOMEONE

RIVER
Tram Crash
19th August 1917
IN COMMEMORATION
OF THE 11 PEOPLE
WHO LOST THEIR
LIVES AND THE
61 INJURED AT
THIS SPOT
THE DOVER SOCIETY

The cemetery came about because, in the 1850s, there were big concerns that because so many people were coming into towns and cities from the country, existing church graveyards were all filling up. So several Municipal Burial Acts were brought in which obliged local authorities to find out-of-town areas for their cemeteries. This was open farmland originally. St James's Cemetery was in one of the two core parishes of Dover, and was the first of four dating from 1855. They choose this site largely because of its beautiful, undulating picturesque nature. It was decided on by one casting vote from the vicar himself, believe it or not.

Princess Anne was here last Tuesday, there's a photo in the national press of her standing by the stone of Gunner Andrew McDowell, who died because of a misheard command. She came with her husband Sir Timothy Laurence and is the patron of the Remembrance Trust. Their aim is the future preservation of military war graves which date from before the First or Second World Wars (which come under the Commonwealth War Graves Commission — anything before that does not). If you died in the Crimean or Boer War, your stone does not qualify under the Commonwealth heading, so this is where the Remembrance Trust comes in.

Photograph: Mary Glow

I was impressed by the light flooding through the Victorian stained-glass windows into the Maison Dieu Stone Hall. I wanted to capture everything in the room, including the colourful windows, scaffolding, building work in progress, and some of the other young photographers, who can be spotted in the foreground in hard hats and high-vis jackets.

This room's seen a lot of history! It's been used by medieval pilgrims as a place to bunk down for the night; as a bakery, making rock-hard ship's biscuit for the Royal Navy; and more recently, as a popular events venue, including for weddings, beer festivals and even a Zombie music video.

I used an 8-15mm fish-eye lens to capture the whole room from the gallery, using photo-editing software to make the image warmer. I've loved taking part in the Maison Dieu project because it's different every time we visit. The whole building is evolving, and it's great to capture this important moment in time. It is due to reopen in summer 2025.

Photograph: Ewan Gartshore

SHRAPNEL HOLE, SHARP & ENRIGHT, SNARGATE STREET

/// HUNTER.FABRIC.LIVID

Sharp & Enright is probably the oldest shop in Dover. My great, great grandfather John Sharp started the business with Mr Enright in 1860 as a ships' chandlers and general merchants.

The business was then passed through the generations to Sidney, who bought the shop at 133 Snargate Street, the property we are in now, in 1928 for £1000; it was a lot of money in those days. The business was then passed to my grandfather John, and then my father Mike, who I worked with daily for 30 years — and now me, Sarah! I enjoy running the business with all its challenges; no day or customer is the same.

The shrapnel hole was part of a large explosion during the Second World War. The story goes that there was a kapok-filled lifejacket on the back of the door and the shrapnel passed though the door and caulked the table in front, also cutting some tennis balls in half.

My great grandfather Sidney was on his own in the shop during the war, it must have been a very frightening time.

Photograph: Amy West

EVERYWHERE MEANS SOMETHING TO SOMEONE

I would like to nominate this building as worthy of note: Maybrook House, which was built in 1964 as an office building. On 21st November 1989 the Dover Royal Naval Auxiliary Service opened it as their new Port Headquarters. As I was the youngest, I was allowed to cut the cake alongside Admiral Sir Jeremy Black. The branch had previously been stationed at the Eastern Docks in the pens, before it was filled in.

The Royal Naval Auxiliary Service was a uniformed, unarmed, civilian volunteer service trained by the Royal Navy to operate in ports and anchorages around the UK, in case of emergency. Unfortunately, defence cuts meant the service was disbanded in 1994.

I received my Long Service Medal in this building in 1993 from Prince Michael of Kent. I am the youngest ever to receive this medal and always will be, due to the disbandment of the service. We had the top floor office, and we did our best to make it a functional Naval HQ. But it will be the ceremonial moments and the last evening we all served together that makes this building one of my favourites in Dover.

Photograph: Mary Glow

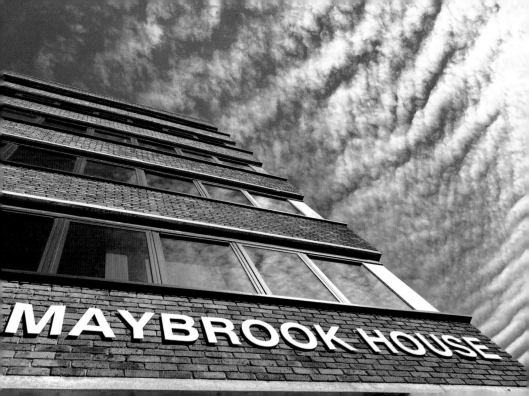

Dover Harbour is a magical meeting place for locals, and for the thousands of visitors who step onto the shingle every year. I rowed with the mighty Dover Rowing Club, the oldest coastal rowing club in the UK, for several years and loved being on the water, observing the seafront from different aspects. The changing light and its power to transform the sea, the cliffs, the Castle, the pier, the seafront in a moment, is both mesmerising and magnificent. During the pandemic I began to swim in the harbour as often as possible and, like many others, continued these swims throughout the year. Almost four years later, I have come to understand that Swimmers' Beach is mecca for long distance swimmers, who head here from all over the world. There is a tangible excitement on the beach during the open water swimming season as swimmers train for their endurance swims. I taught myself how to do front crawl by watching these swimmers and then practicing. There is so much experience and hope and dreams on the beach and in the water; it is thrilling, and it is home.

Photograph: Rebecca Sperini

EVERYWHERE MEANS SOMETHING TO SOMEONE

THE PRINCE ALBERT, BIGGIN STREET

Our paternal grandparents Bill and Maggie ran the Prince Albert until 1971. As you walked in the main entrance, there was a corridor and a staircase — under the stairs was access to the cellar. To the right was the main bar, and to the left was a room with a piano, which we could play when the pub was closed. It was a meeting room for The Order of Buffaloes; it had a buffalo head in the cupboard by the fireplace. I don't know if it was a stuffed head or just a prop. In our day, the toilets were outside, and behind the main bar was a small private snug.

The whole family used to spend Christmas there. My brother and I slept in the bathroom, top and tailed in a single brass feather bed, while the turkey was covered over with a tea towel on a chest of drawers. My dad and uncle helped Granddad out behind the bar, and Grandma cooked the dinner ready for 3 o'clock when the pub closed.

I try to pop in for a pint a couple of times a year. I find it quite nostalgic sitting there reliving my childhood memories.

Photograph: Strange Cargo

EVERYWHERE MEANS SOMETHING TO SOMEONE

This memorial here and the one next to it, you can't really read it, but it's to members of the Knocker family. They lived in Castle Hill House, a Grade II listed building dating from 1760, close to the White Horse public house. The Knockers were Town Clerks for three generations. The stone on the left commemorates Edward Knocker, who was the first of the three Town Clerks, and next door is Sir Edward Wollaston-Knocker, whose grave is sadly in a terrible condition. He's said to be the only Town Clerk in the country to have been knighted. It's through Sir Edward that Dover transformed itself from the industrial revolution time into the modern age; he was responsible for the naming of a lot of streets that were put down in the development from the 1880s onward. He was also behind the introduction of a tram network, and all sorts of big, grand projects boiled down to this man here. Then his son was Reginald Edward Knocker, who was the last... he finished in 1936 I think it was. These three more or less ran Dover, even though they were not elected representatives.

Photograph: Amy West

The last enemy-fired shell to land on Dover destroyed shops in Castle Street just yards from the town's Market Square. The shell, fired from the French coast, crashed down on 26th September 1944. It was the last of more than 2,000 German missiles to hit the borough since 1940.

More than a thousand properties were wrecked by the shells which came down, as well as enemy bombs. The people of Dover never knew when the next shell was coming. As a result, Dover's pre-war population of around 43,000 sank to a few thousand. It never returned to its pre-1939 population, but has since hovered around the 30,000 mark.

More than 3000 children were evacuated from Dover, by special train in June 1940, just as the survivors of the Dunkirk Evacuation were arriving at the Docks. The Dover children, a few aged six years old, came from a range of schools, and were found new homes, mostly in South Wales. There some of them remained until Christmas 1944. Most were carefully looked after with love by their Welsh hosts and foster parents. A few had a rough time.

Photograph: Susan Pilcher

EVERYWHERE MEANS SOMETHING TO SOMEONE

DETACHED BASTIONS, WESTERN HEIGHTS

This is my memory of exploring the Detached Bastions on the Western Heights, some of the abandoned forts and overgrown moats of Dover. It started off with some light obstacles that became progressively more precarious. Although not too long ago, my memory of the exact sequence of events is imperfect. I recall sliding under a fence, passing the skeleton of a bridge and running down into a ditch — the first of many.

A small amount of traversing brambles and stepping over empty cans before we arrived at tall walls, covered in graffiti. The fort is huge, with a multitude of openings filled in, destroyed and filled in again. There are makeshift ladders, piles of stones and hanging ropes to help you access hard to reach areas. The experience is very layered — you're climbing high off the ground, yet somehow feel buried beneath the town. We started off by exploring the overgrowth. Passing stone archways, small windows and debris-blocked tunnels with ominous words spray painted above.

There's a suspenseful energy to the place. You're remote and removed, but one turn of a corner and you've encountered an abandoned washing machine. I remember getting stung and scratched by nettles and thorns, and leaving sore with a muddy bum and an undoubtable adrenaline high.

Photograph: Rebecca Sperini

My father was half French and we had lots of family in northern France. We were especially close to my second cousins — four boys around the same age as me and my sister. They'd come to visit, often camping near our home in rural Kent.

I recall many trips to Dover, seeing them off back to Calais or Boulogne where they'd all get on a train back home to Lille. Sometimes their friends would come too. I was exceptionally lucky in my early teens having so many French boys as friends — and some as potential boyfriends! I fondly remember Christian and Pierre, as well as my favourite cousin Yves, we had some great times.

This was 1973, 74 and 75 — the world and our ways of communicating were very different then! I remember standing on the Dock, seeing them onto the ferry. It could get quite emotional — I was a hormonal teen after all!

Photograph: Rebecca Sperini

My son's year three primary school teacher Miss Allen was passionate about Roman history, which was conveniently on the national curriculum in the '90s.

Miss Allen arranged class trips to the Roman Painted House every year, and I would take time off work to go along as a parent helper when both my boys' classes went. For them to see things from their history books with their own eyes was incredible. At seven years old they absolutely loved it — plus, it was a sneaky way to feed my own Roman history habit!

....

The Roman Painted House is the finest Roman house on show in Britain; it was discovered by Kent Archaeological Rescue Unit. 40 years of excavation across ancient Dover by the Unit have uncovered 50 major structures. The Painted House was the best preserved, and is now a major tourist attraction. Built in about AD 200, it formed part of a large mansion or official hotel, for travellers crossing the Channel. It stood outside the great naval fort of the Classis Britannica, but in AD 270 it was demolished by the Roman army during the construction of a larger fort.

Photograph: Strange Cargo

Cecil Rhodes was a tattoo artist, sign writer, photographer, and driver in the Army.

He tattooed throughout both World Wars, both tattooing troops whilst posted out, and running his own studio on Snargate Street in Dover.

Snargate Street is opposite the Marina and has historically had a large footfall of sailors seeking tattoos. Cecil's studio was bombed and destroyed in WW2, but many of his flash sheets and machines have been saved.

I opened Harbourside Tattoo on Snargate Street a couple of years ago. The area has so much history, and our building is Grade Two listed. I'm a traditional tattooist, and the fact that Cecil Rhodes used to work on this very street sealed the deal for me.

Photograph: Rebecca Sperini

EMMAUS

There are 13 Emmaus branches in Britain at the moment — there's a couple of new ones up in Oxford, which are looking forward to being completed. Basically, they're all round the world: the whole idea is to give homeless people a home, and the shops and the furniture, the garden centre, everything here basically, the warehouses, are all geared to raising funds to help the residents. All the people that have homes at Emmaus are called Companions. Staff members come in during the week and do what they need to do with the shop. There's a kitchen, cookers, freezer, all stocked up. Some of the people that live here come from as far as Cornwall, Somerset, loads of places; they come here because they're homeless. This is all an old fortress along here. There's a gymnasium, with some weights and things, and original stables as well.

Emmaus asks for donations — it can be anything basically, as long as it's got a fire label, we take it. It's basically the cheapest place in this country to get second-hand goods, they've got an department that they do Pat testing on electrical items. Matthew is here, he does upholstery. They've put new stained-glass windows in the shop. They're taking good care of the place.

Photograph: Strange Cargo

EVERYWHERE MEANS SOMETHING TO SOMEONE

I used to be a tour manager for punk bands. After a big night in Paris, we drove overnight to the Calais ferry. We found some seats to lay our weary heads and drifted off to sleep. One of the members of the band, who had had a good amount to drink, realised he'd forgotten to get his girlfriend a gift while he'd been away. He decided he would go to the ferry's gift shop and get her a teddy. After choosing a particularly fluffy pink one, he returned in his drunken stupor to his sleep spot.

A while later, he was awoken by the P&O staff demanding his passport. He handed it over and was immediately accused of shoplifting, as he had failed to pay for the teddy. Myself and the rest of the band were woken up by this commotion, as the staff proceeded to take the situation incredibly seriously. We were finding it difficult not to laugh, as we looked on while our dishevelled, large northern friend was being told off. The staff called the police and refused to let us leave the terminal, adamant there would be an arrest. Fortunately, when the police arrived, they also saw the funnier side and, after having a decent laugh at us, they let us go, albeit without the pink fluffy teddy.

Photograph: Rebecca Sperini

As a little girl, my grandad would take me and my brother to Kearsney Abbey in his Morris Minor. We would pack up a picnic, paddle in the water, feed the swans, have an ice cream, and then walk across the road to the Russell Gardens play park.

Grandad would tell us about the types of trees and birds around us. We'd play games and enjoy quality time together. My grandad later went into a care home due to dementia and suffering from a stroke. I would take him back there and we'd just sit. He was unable to speak but I could tell from his eyes that he remembered where we were.

When I had my own kids, I would take them to enjoy the place. I go there to clear my head and can still feel the presence of my grandad, it's truly a special place to me.

Photograph: Strange Cargo

As a teenager I used to enjoy exploring abandoned buildings. There was a forum on the internet called 28DaysLater, where I connected with three strangers who shared this interest. We chatted online about exploring the Detached Bastion and decided to meet up at Dover station. At no point prior to this had we discussed our ages, and I think they were a bit surprised when I, a borderline child, showed up. After the initial shock they were lovely about it, and took me under their wing.

We went to the Detached Bastion where we spent a number of hours taking photos and exploring the ruins. At one point we heard footsteps approaching, it was other members of the public exploring the fortress. One of the guys I was with said, "Watch this," and proceeded to put on a military-style gas mask. He hid around the corner as the strangers approached, jumped out and screamed at them. They ran away and he proceeded to chase them, screaming. I wasn't sure whether to laugh or cry.

Photograph: Simon Bill

I remember sneaking down the alleyway by Astor school, to bunk off maths and go to my friend's house to eat snacks and watch horror movies.

We would run from school, and by the time we got to the alleyway we would be so puffed out but laughing, because we knew we were safely out of sight at that point.

We were obsessed with the *Amityville Horror* and, when you're 13 years old and watching a certificate 18 film, it's the ultimate experience.

Photograph: Rebecca Sperini

On Castle Hill Road there are a series of short cycle lanes, some only eight metres long. As a driving instructor I'd pass them and wonder about the reasoning behind them. Rumour has it each new cycle lane would receive £2000 funding, with an additional £50 per a metre. I've spotted at least 38 around which, in addition to teaching people to drive, provides an excellent maths lesson.

Photograph: Rebecca Sperini

DOVER DARLINGS SWIM CLUB

I started sea swimming on my own, and later joined the Dover Darlings. I suffer from psoriasis, and the sea water helps both my skin and my mental health. It gives me such a feeling of being uplifted. The Dover Darlings is an amazing group, I wouldn't be doing it without them now. I swim off Swimmers' Beach, behind the seafood stand and up by the clock tower.

I fit swimming in between working and the school run, and meet with the group on the weekend. I'd love to do a sunrise swim. I've done a full moon swim — such a wonderful experience. There is no better feeling than being out in the water, hearing the boats, with the birds for company and looking back at the Castle.

Lots of people contact us about first time swimming and, to anyone new to sea swimming, I would recommend contacting us. It's easier to start in the winter and swim into the warmer temperatures. If you're going to start in the winter then make sure you have plenty of layers and a warm drink afterwards, but it is the natural high you get from cold water that is the best bit, and being with like-minded people.

Photograph: Rebecca Sperini

EVERYWHERE MEANS SOMETHING TO SOMEONE

I've been here many times to see live bands, and all have been really enjoyable nights out. There's always a good crowd of people, all there to enjoy the music. For me the Booking Hall has a good mix of cover bands, local bands, and the occasional more known bands. Some of the bigger acts have been Frank Turner, Dragonforce, The Sugerhill Gang, Skies, Wheatus, Don Bronco, Skindred... just the few I've managed to see.

Being a small independent music venue, it has tried to showcase local up and coming bands, giving them a bigger platform to play on, which I think is beneficial for any band that wants to try something a bit bigger than their local pub. A regular notable local band I've seen is one called Wicked Stone. A few other local bands have also been opening acts for some of the bigger bands.

There's been a lot mentioned recently about trying to keep grassroots venues going. It just shows what the community can do, when they want to save something they love. Hopefully the Booking Hall will stay for many more years to come, so it can keep being enjoyed and be the go-to place for live music.

Photograph: Rebecca Sperini

I lived up on Astor Avenue and we were playing football in the road. There used to be a place, a hall... and down either side there was a brick wall and a path and in between the wall and the path was a drop of about six feet. I was standing on the wall, someone kicked the football, and I trapped it with my foot and fell down in the gap. My arm went *bang*, and broke in four places. Bones poking this way and that, another bit going another direction.

I didn't feel any pain yet. I walked home and dad was just finishing his tea and reading the paper, and when he looked at me he went, "What have you done to your arm?" We walked to Victoria Hospital. My dad told the doctor, "He's eaten his tea and half of my tea too," so the doctor told us we'd have to wait until I had an empty stomach to set my arm. So, we waited until midnight.

I got away with doing nothing for about six weeks at school until an old biddy of a teacher found out I was left handed.

Photograph: Rebecca Sperini

I had started a new job, working for a private healthcare company based in offices above the beauty salon in Bench Street. It was my second week there and I needed to get some keys cut, so I made my way up Cannon Street through Market Square on a cold Tuesday morning at about 10am, heading to Timpson's, and my journey took me past a well-known pub. When I was within 100m of said pub, the doors burst open and four men in their late 50s spilled onto the pavement and proceeded to have an almighty dust-up, complete with a high volume of imaginative profanity. I stopped and watched, obviously, and then realised that there were two other men sat in a ringside position on the pub's outside tables enjoying the whole event, each drinking a pint of Stella. Eventually the fight subsided, two of the men went back into the pub and the other two headed down the road shouting further obscenities as they went.

I got my keys cut and returned to the office to regale my new colleagues with my experience. Nobody seemed surprised.

Photograph: Strange Cargo

If I was going to recommend anywhere for people, I think it would be Dover Transport Museum: it's a great place to visit, and your initial ticket price gets you in for the rest of the year. It's at the top of Whitfield Hill and is a brilliant place and packs a lot in.

There are displays from the 19th and 20th centuries, and many different types of transport-related exhibits, including tanks and a steam train. You see lots of families there, but it also appeals to people who really like transport history. From what I know, they have events throughout the year, and they do stuff for children, you know, Easter egg hunts and Christmas events. They seem to add to their collection quite regularly. You can potter round for ages, it's fascinating, and there's a café too if you want a cup of tea and a nice jammy scone. They quite often have classic car or classic motorbike events too for owners to join in. I really enjoy going there and think more people should know about it. They're on social media, so check them out. There's nowhere else like it anywhere in the area. It's best to check their opening times online as they're not open every day.

Photograph: Amy West

It's the uniqueness of Dover that people can sometimes miss. There was all this wealth, there was a lot in the 18th and 19th centuries, and people built all these amazing buildings and the mills... and everyone that had a mill had a posh house next to it, many of which are still around, and no one is really aware of why that really nice house is sitting right next to a council estate. Of course, the council estate was built on the old mill site. I'm thinking about the old lumber yard at the bottom of my road, as you go out of Dover and go past the Buckland Hospital road, and that little stretch up to the Buckland Bridge, where it curves, on your right, there's a beautiful house which was owned by the bloke that had the lumber mill that was on this site, so on that corner there was a big lumber yard with an arch over it. Its all modern housing now. On the edge of one of the poorest estates in the country is that a beautiful house, which I think is now a care home. But there's always this juxtaposition in Dover.

Photograph: Strange Cargo

On 18th July 2012 the Olympic torch came through Dover. I volunteered to be part of this historic moment. All the volunteers assembled at the sports centre and were sorted into teams and given high-viz vests and baseball caps — not my usual attire! All excited and raring to go. I stood on the Ladywell route, and once the torch had passed, we went to cover Castle Street, and then to the seaside end of the underpass. We were there to greet people going to the ticketed celebrations and then wave them off, after the fireworks.

There were huge crowds expected, but the weather was filthy. It rained and we got soaked. However, standing in the downpour on Ladywell as the torch bearer came past was amazing and, despite the rain, people lined the streets and everyone was smiling and cheering.

The TV covered the spectacular parts of the relay: the arrival of the torch by sailing boat, the Castle, the lighting of the cauldron. There was real heart in the whole event, people were delighted to be part of something big, and thrilled that Dover was the focus of something so positive. There was a real pride in our town on that day.

Photograph: Rebecca Sperini

We arrived in the dark, huddled in the back of a removal van. Our mum had told us it was just a row of houses with fields for miles, there would be a fairy castle, and that the seaside was just five minutes away. I realised pretty sharpish that she had coloured this in a little when we finally saw daylight. My two brothers, my baby sister, alongside Mum and I, were all stood at the back of the removal van at the bottom of Barwick Road. I saw not just a few houses, but a whole estate, surrounded either side by hills. The fairy castle, though impressive, did not hold Sleeping Beauty within, and the beach was not literally on our doorstep.

We joked with her for years about that. This town was going to be home for the next 20 years, and in 2001 I left. Then, in 2011, I returned, and this time in the front seat of the removal van. We approached from the road that passes Aycliffe and saw the Castle. I heard a "Wow!" coming from my friends who'd been helping me that day, "Whatever made you leave this? Dover is lovely," they said. And they're right.

Photograph: Rebecca Sperini

My favourite part of Dover has to be Western Heights. In 1995, when I was only 15, every one of my 15-year-old friends said they had been to an illegal rave, or knew someone who ran one. Upon further questioning, quite quickly I established they were talking nonsense. I was quite dubious when a friend of a friend said she knew of one that was going on and did we want to go. Later on that evening I'm crawling across a bridge over a moat into the Drop Redoubt, full of excitement. Originally built for defence purposes to keep Napoleon at bay, that night was the stage for my first illegal rave with my best pal. I remember what I was wearing (MA2 flight jacket and Levis), how we danced all night, how awful it was walking back down to the station at 8am, and how my friends wouldn't believe us (we didn't care). You can now go inside on certain open days — check English Heritage. It's still a lovely walk around the fort though, looking down to the port across to France.

Photograph: Rebecca Sperini

I work in Maison Dieu Road in Dover and I can see the Castle from my desk, which is not a view many can boast. Dover Castle is part of English Heritage too, and really worth a visit. The lighthouse is a great walk and you can park in the National Trust car park where they have a fab tea and cake.

Make sure to visit the Kent Bakery on London Road. My synopsis of Dover: great walks, wonderful buildings, with a banging bakery.

Photograph: Rebecca Sperini

Flapjack
70p

Bakewell
Slice 70p

Carmel
Slice 75p

Belgian
Bun 70p

Iced bun
65p

Sausage roll
& two mix
2. hot two

For me, the most iconic place or view in Dover is the glorious White Cliffs. The perfect place to go, to stand in awe at the beauty of the world and blow away the cobwebs on a good walk. I've even run across there before with my local Dover running club. I've visited many a time with friends and family and it's always a joy.

My most special, memorable experience happened there in 2018. It was a Sunday, and the weather was just a tad grey! So cloudy and a little windy, but my husband insisted that we should head up there for our walk; I thought he was mad but obliged as he seemed so keen. I'm so glad I did, as it's the exact spot where he asked me to be his wife!

I think what makes the White Cliffs so special is they've stood the test of time. Standing there, looking out to sea, or back towards the Castle, I think how this is the same view that people have seen for a thousand years, and it is the same view that our grandchildren will have. We are the custodians of it, and it is our duty to preserve it for the next generations.

Photograph: Sophie Jessup

Dover Athletic, for many, is the centre of the community. Football can be a focal point, offering an opportunity for entertainment or recreation. You'll see groups of people walking through town towards Crabble, all with the same intention, to have some fun and let off steam. It's an opportunity to meet up with mates, have a few beers and escape the usual realities of everyday life.

But for me, it was something I did with my grandad. For as long as I could remember we went together. It's probably the biggest thing that we bonded over. I saw a quote recently that said, 'Attending live football games throughout my life has been the pin that connects me with the men in my family.' This was very true for us. He died in late November 2019, a few months before Covid started. Covid caused major difficulties for the club, which has since seen a period of decline.

The death of my grandad and the club's difficulties coincided, and to me the loss almost feels related. Since then, I've volunteered my time to the club as Media Officer. It gives me a real sense of purpose and helps me remember the good times I shared with my grandad and the club.

Photograph: George Cory

EVERYWHERE MEANS SOMETHING TO SOMEONE

Coconut madeleine and a strawberry milkshake at Elizabeth's — the scent of coffee in there was heady — I loved it. And going shopping with Nan meant waiting in every single shop while she chatted with the shopkeepers and other customers. There was a bentwood chair in many shops, but they were "for ladies, not children"... so I stood, quietly bored, in the wool shop, the butchers, and the fishmongers with their tangy scent and sawdust on the floor. The odds and sods shop that sold things like lightbulbs, pegs, etc; the antique shop... all in baby-sized little shops round the sides of the Market Hall. Gutteridge, the chemist in the Market Square, had huge flasks of emerald green and ruby red coloured water in the window; the shop is curved and sits just where Biggin Street goes from the Market Square, and was entirely fitted in wonderful dark wood panelling and counters with glazed cabinets for perfume etc. Hatton's for ribbons, elastic, buttons and lace. At Payne's, the veg shop, it ponged of boiled beetroot. Rook's on the High Street, and Wendy's, the wool shop in Worthington Street — listening to much the same gossip in each shop.

Photograph: Susan Pilcher

EVERYWHERE MEANS SOMETHING TO SOMEONE

The fort was built in Edward VI's time I think; there was Roman stuff here before. It's really ancient and all the buildings are listed. The archaeology people have been here and found guns and shells; they found a body before, when they first started, over where the houses are, they dug up the bones of some people. I don't think they were very old. There was a big house here, where that red and white sign is, and those two pillars are all that remains of it. The only reason it's that's not there now is that Jerry dropped a bomb on it in the Second World War.

This site has taken some damage, and has been on the front line of many conflicts. They expected to close the gate and keep the enemy out, so there are water stores underground, ammunition stores beneath the carpark; we've had an archaeologist down there on a ladder, it goes down 12 feet, under that metal cover, and there's a lovely building underground. We're not troubled by the sea, we're lucky in that way as we've got a bit of distance, although it gets a bit salty up here.

Photograph: Strange Cargo

There have been over 200 patches of original William Burgess painted decoration uncovered during the restoration of the Maison Dieu. In the Mayor's Parlour, which is a really high-status room, there is a giant American walnut table with eighteen legs. It was too big and heavy to take out of the room during the restoration. The room has a decorative ceiling that was originally painted by William Burgess on strips of canvas which were then applied. He loved medieval animals, so we've got two-legged dragons and, on the corbels, there are birds of prey; it looks like a hawk. The painted niches: the story goes that the virtues were painted in the niches on canvas, but later removed and replaced with 1960s wallpaper, a copy of Pugin wallpaper. The original design was done in the 1850s for the Houses of Parliament, but this is a later version.

During the Second World War a German shell dropped on the fire station across the road and didn't explode, but a piece of shrapnel came through the window and embedded itself in that table; it's still there — a big chunk! The shell was fired from the coast of France, and if it had gone off this building wouldn't be here today.

Photograph: Martin Crowther

EVERYWHERE MEANS SOMETHING TO SOMEONE

KEARSNEY ABBEY

When my daughter was about six years old I remember finding a plaque at the south eastern end of the Abbey lake, commemorating somebody who died in a massacre. The plaque, now faded, was clearer 40 years ago. It reads something like, 'in memory of ... who was cruelly massacred ...'. My daughter brilliantly read out the entire plaque, but misread one of the words as 'massaged'. Not being such a brilliant parent, I'm afraid I laughed and laughed, and today I still smile when I think of that moment. She was such a precious child.

Photograph: Susan Pilcher

EVERYWHERE MEANS SOMETHING TO SOMEONE

I was standing on the pier where the new Wellington Marina is, when a bird's head poked above the water. I wasn't the only one that spotted the bird and thought it was a penguin. They looked very similar.

It was swimming between the new marina berths. I was with my two year old daughter and my wife Jodie at the time.

I was sure it couldn't be a penguin being so far south, but I did do a double take!

Photograph: Strange Cargo

My first tattooist in Dover was Nick, who was a Hell's Angel and ran a salon called Merlin's, which is still around. Nick unfortunately died horrifically on Whitfield Hill. I then went to the chap that had taken over Merlin's, called Sean.

I was Mayor during the 70th anniversary of the Battle of Britain and I talked to a lot of veterans, who told me so much about that time, and I was so impressed that I got a Spitfire and the White Cliffs of Dover tattooed on my arm. Now, I go to Dave Bruce's salon at Pins and Needles, by the Eagle pub. All my recent work is done there, including one for my mum, who I lost a couple of years ago. When I started work, tattoos had to be covered and I wouldn't have got jobs if I hadn't been able to cover them up. But now, we're a much freer society and I can express myself openly. Pretty much all of them have a meaning somewhere: I have this Celtic design for my former Mayoress Ronnie — she was my Mayoress twice and she passed away; she was a Christian but she loved the whole Celtic thing.

Photograph: David Bruce

I know from speaking to the thousands of tourists that came to buy ice cream from me that people are friendly and love to talk about the place. Tourism has changed. Pre-Covid there were Dutch — hundreds of Dutch visitors — American, Japanese, very distinctive. The Japanese and Americans would have a once in a lifetime trip to the UK; they would always come and look at the White Cliffs of Dover — the whole *blue birds* thing.

The Dutch, I suppose we're far enough away for it to be a holiday, but not so far away that they can't get here easily. Rarely French visitors, and sometime Spanish. The Japanese, they eat up our culture. I would get asked five times a day, "How do I get to the White Cliffs of Dover?" There's still a bit of driftwood on the ice cream kiosk which says White Cliffs half kilometre that way!

This always makes me smile when I think about it: apparently, the ancient Britons stood on the cliffs, when the harbour was literally where the Market Square is, and repelled the Roman invaders by throwing rocks off the cliff, so the Romans went up to Reculver instead.

Photograph: Mary Glow

The cedar of Lebanon at Kearsney Abbey is said to be the oldest of its kind in the country. It's now fenced off due to a lean and the danger of falling limbs, but it's still very much alive. This heritage tree is very distinctive, with far spreading branches and enormous height — it feels as high as a ten story building. Whether that's accurate, I don't know.

Kearsney Abbey was built 160 years ago, and it's believed that the cedar of Lebanon was planted at this time. Its close proximity to a rare chalk stream makes for an environment which feels truly special.

It's a tree with Biblical connotations, revered by civilisations for thousands of years. I love that this middle eastern tree, the oldest in the country, belongs to Dover.

....

This was our place on a Sunday morning, taking the grandparents' dog for a walk. Catching sticklebacks with nets and feeding the ducks and swans. I used to climb the large Lebanese cedar that is now fenced off. It was a great tree to climb. I heard that it was one of the oldest, but not sure how old it actually is. It had a wonderful full scented smell.

Photograph: Strange Cargo

EVERYWHERE MEANS SOMETHING TO SOMEONE

My grandfather spent some time here when he was sent off in the First World War. He was local, and quite a bit of our family spent some time here, but it's come to be quite a bit different in modern times. All these walls, they're all original walls — that's an ex-guardhouse over there, next to the archway, which is where the military guards were posted, keeping out civilians and the enemy. It was a proper military establishment, all very strict and run properly, and they looked out for each other.

You can't get down to the seafront from here now. It does go further, but it's underground, under this concrete piece they've just done in the carpark. Under there is an older shelter of some kind that leads out to the seafront. Well, because the fort was actually made to be a sea fort, and it was massive, it actually extended all the way to the seafront where that pile of rocks is now, but it got demolished because the train needed to go through. The railway runs along the seafront through to Dover Priory.

Photograph: Strange Cargo

There were lots of B&B's, and people often wanted a bed for one night, but Dover wasn't a destination for the week, it was always part of a bigger tour of anything interesting in East Kent. And because we're so well connected in Kent, it was really easy and quick, you could do Canterbury Cathedral, you could do the White Cliffs of Dover, Leeds Castle and then back into London.

....

One of the funniest descriptions of Dover that I have ever read was by Bill Bryson recalling his visit to the town in 1973 in his book *Notes from a Small Island*; a little caustic, but having grown up with parents who ran a B&B it was very close to the truth. His first night was spent on a bench in a seafront shelter and, by the sounds of it, it may very well have been this one.

Photograph: Susan Pilcher

This is the stairwell at the Charlton Shopping Centre that Future Foundry is turning into an exhibition space. There are light boxes mounted on the wall and we exhibit photography, and have turned it into a proper exhibition space. I think it works really well because the surroundings, the tiles and floor, are kind of dated, and using light boxes in a way is dated too, because people tend to use screens now. It's a dark space with not much natural light, so the artworks really pop. It really works.

The photos are printed on translucent paper, which we mount on the boxes. It's a rotating exhibition which is currently Dover Youth Festival. We do a lot of work in schools, and we ran a cultural survey in schools which inspired Dover Youth Festival, which then led to this exhibition space.

Photograph: Rebecca Sperini

EVERYWHERE MEANS SOMETHING TO SOMEONE

BUBBLE TEA BASE

You can get bubble tea in Dover, do you know by the graveyard, and you go down that street, there's Panda Bubble Tea there. It's the only place to get it in Dover. I maybe saw it in Costa once, but it wasn't proper bubble tea.

You can get different flavours, like milk ones and fruit ones. I get whatever my friend from school gets because then I get to try different flavours each time. You can also get milkshakes from there. But it's the bubble tea why we go.

Photograph: Susan Pilcher

I am a filmmaker currently making a documentary about the restoration of the Maison Dieu and the community workshops that happen inside. Each time I return I discover another set of eyes watching me from the walls within, or on the external stonework. It's very exciting to see the discoveries being uncovered through the layers of decoration and building work, which in turn reveal layers of history. It's magical to see inside the skeleton of the building, and to imagine the people and activities that have occurred since the medieval times.

The face inside the Council Chamber looks down upon you, its eyes following you wherever you go. It certainly makes you feel like you are not alone and made me reflect on the intimidating and sometimes cruel attitudes of the past. I filmed the rooftop grotesque, from the scaffolding which currently surrounds the building. To be able to get this close and study the careful detail felt like a once in a lifetime opportunity and an immense privilege. On close inspection its features are weathered. This made me consider the environmental impact on the stonework, our history and lives.

Photograph: Alex Davies

My favourite place near Dover is Kearsney Abbey and Russell Gardens.

Even before I had my little Lhasa Apso dog, I would always take out of town relatives and visitors to the Abbey and to Russell Gardens. It was a favourite place to take my daughter and sometimes go with her friends. The swans are always diverting and at the weekends, watching the boats on the southeastern end of the Abbey lake would be a lovely distraction.

With dogs allowed off the lead on the southwestern side of the lake, it provides a perfect balance to the opposite side, where swans roam freely, but dogs must be kept on a lead. Here there is also a splendid tearoom, which certainly used to sell tea and ice cream at a reasonable price, and I think still does, even since its refurbishment.

Photograph: Strange Cargo

Dover is brilliant from a natural history point of view for plants and animals, because we're so close to the Continent. The plants that are here in the chalk grassland probably at one time grew on the cliff face. The clifftop grassland originally stayed that way because the salt spray kills other things off, so it's less likely to have scrub growing.

Chalk grassland plants like open habitat, and prehistoric people were thought to have cleared the forests after the Ice Age to create grazing for animals. Big herbivores would have taken down trees and grubbed up areas; there used to be aurochs, and further back, elephants. There was woodland after the last Ice Age, but gradually that got cleared and plants spread into areas where there wasn't shade. So, I'd say the chalk grassland that we've got has been affected by mankind with grazing animals, and it's that grazing pressure that helps keep shrubs and trees under control and keep the variety and biodiversity of plants. It's because of grazing, the animals suppress the very coarse grasses and bushes, allowing all the little herbs and orchids to grow, and for the area to remain open grassland.

Photograph: © The Trustees of the
Natural History Museum, London

CHALK GRASSLAND

© BRITISH MUSEUM (NATURAL HISTORY)

These bricked-up areas around the entrance are gun-points, they used to have guns pointing out. Everywhere there's a lintel, there used to be a gun. The flint shards in the lime mortar are to deter anyone from trying to get in, making it as difficult as possible to dislodge the brickwork. To the right of the entrance is the moat, there's entrances here, there, and everywhere. It was built for concealment, so nobody knew it was there, especially if they'd landed on the beach. It was designed to be a hidden fort and was allowed to get overgrown. Everything was built for a purpose and then was concealed, so it wouldn't be discovered if the enemy was landing anywhere. Invaders couldn't get in anyway, 'cause once they got to a moat like that, they couldn't get across it. It was a dry moat and it had bomb disposal buildings in there; I've found stuff down there from bomb disposal crews and, of course, they had the best of the best people to do what they had to do. So, they were definitely exploring lots of different things up there, trying lots of new things. Innovation was part of it, as it was the only way to get advanced and to win a war, I guess.

Photograph: Strange Cargo

EVERYWHERE MEANS SOMETHING TO SOMEONE

We have a bunker. We have multiple bunkers. We don't own them, like, physically, we don't have a certificate, but we go and play there, so mentally we've taken over them and they're ours.

They're up on the Danes, on the eastern slopes of Dover, there's football pitches and stuff there. Anyway, there's two bunkers near each other. You can climb on top of them, then there's a massive hill going up, with loads of pieces of metal, near the graveyard.

We're out exploring and things most Saturdays after youth club, adventuring and stuff. One time Lincoln hid in a bunker and Kai went in to have a look around in the dark, Lincoln was round this corner and jumped out and it was so funny because Kai proper screamed.

Photograph: Susan Pilcher

EVERYWHERE MEANS SOMETHING TO SOMEONE

I worked at an event at Fort Burgoyne once, it all came about because of a Pioneering Places project. I can't remember all of their names, but one is called Peter Cocks. Him and these other guys set up this group called Albion Incorporated, that tried to do something, tried to do some placemaking in Dover, in response to the Pioneering Places project.

It then became like a Fort Burgoyne open day, that was kind of conceived as a way of showing its possible use. Trying to imagine what it could be used for, what could be done with it. So, it had lots of art stuff going on, Future Foundry was there, the Folklore Museum was there, putting stuff on in the space.

They themed it around this thing called 'Waking the Giant' because there were old giant puppets, kind of similar to Little Amal and that style of big puppet. There was the framework of a giant that had been donated by Strange Cargo and I don't know who those other puppets even were. I think the whole thing came about because they were in a shed at Fort Burgoyne.

Photograph: Susan Pilcher

EVERYWHERE MEANS SOMETHING TO SOMEONE

Fort Burgoyne

It all stems from having free bus passes as teenagers. We would all just get on buses to places, and one day we went to Dover. My friend was like, "My uncle has a boat in the marina," the one just as you're coming into Dover on the right before you get to St James's.

I slid under the gate and unlocked it from the inside. Then we just went on his boat. I don't even know what we did, we were just on the boat. We must have done it like two or three times, we'd go out on the outboard rig thing and go around the marina on it. It's like a rubber dingy with a little engine on it. I don't know why no one ever said anything, because we were just driving around the marina.

One time the petrol ran out on that, so we had to row it back to the boat. Obviously, the next time his uncle used it he must have thought, "Where's the petrol?"

We took it to the next level once, because we went without our friend whose uncle it was. I remember thinking, "Well now there's zero legitimacy to this day."

Photograph: Susan Pilcher

EVERYWHERE MEANS SOMETHING TO SOMEONE

I started Southeast Gulls Disability FC In 2015. We are based at Farthinglow training ground and train 1-3pm every Sunday. Dover is such a large area that it required opportunities for non-mainstream football, as lots couldn't attend other groups. So, I decided to start a new club. We had two amazing coaches, who were DBS and FA qualified in safeguarding and first aid. Once I found a pitch, I registered our name, affiliated, insurance was sorted, and started the big public relations exercise to find players.

We have a great family club, with so much success, we have recently bought a new kit thanks to an amazing new sponsorship deal with the Port of Dover this month. In May 2019 our juniors won the Chelsea Foundation Shield, which meant they played on Chelsea training ground. And our adult team played at Stamford Bridge, which was a fantastic experience. My coach Robert Barrett won Kent FA Grassroots Coach of the Year in 2019.

We have won Kent Disability League many times, and are currently first place in the premiership. Our new minibus gets us to tournaments. Every player has their own unique needs, and everyone takes this into consideration and helps everyone out.

Photograph: Susan Pilcher

Dover's history has always been determined by its crucial location on the English Channel, just over 20 miles away from France. From Bronze Age boats to Caesar's Romans, the Battle of Britain and cross-Channel ferries, the separation of Dover from Europe by the Channel is a fundamental part of the town's history.

450,000 years ago there was no Channel, and you could continue walking from where the White Cliffs now stand all the way across to France on a ridge of chalk hills. Around this time, arguably the foundational event in the history of Dover occurred — a huge mega-flood overwhelmed the chalk hills, with unimaginable quantities of water spilling over from the area of the North Sea and permanently opening the Strait of Dover and fundamentally shaping the town. Dover Castle, Western Heights and other historic military buildings; the cultural significance of the White Cliffs; the commercial importance of the port; the biodiversity of the surrounding hills and river Dour; all of these and more can be linked back to the mega-flood, which scientists have only in recent years been able to prove occurred. This is one of the most important elements of the new cross-Channel Geopark, which celebrates the shared heritage of our cross-Channel regions that has built up over millions of years.

www.crosschannelgeopark.org

Photograph: © Chase Stone / Imperial College London

Even by the Bronze Age it was quite an open habitat on the cliffs. On Whinless Down there are two sets of Bronze Age burial mounds. They're known as *tumuli* — they're marked on Ordnance Survey maps. It's such a high, steep hill that the archaeologist said that these white burial mounds would've been made of chalk and they would've been seen for miles around. I think that the burial mounds were indicating where the tribes lived, because in the Bronze Age they started burying the elite of the tribe in burial mounds. Before that, in the Stone Age, they had communal burials — it's one of the things that marks the change in culture. They dug out the chalk and buried their people there. Then they had these bowl barrows, pudding shaped, you can just see the mounds up there. In the past we've cleared the scrub over them, so they are grassland now and easier to see. There are so many of them in East Kent, and unfortunately some have been ploughed over the years, but the ones on Whinless Down are still domes.

Photograph: Mary Glow

My friend and I walked from Dover to Dundee, picking up litter. We picked up 10,100 facemasks, plus 800 disposable vapes. Litter is omnipresent, but people don't act. We slept at the First and Last backpackers' hostel in Dover. This guy, Stuart, from the White Horse, made it happen. We had no money, we were litter picking; the whole trip cost us like £1000.

The First and Last is a youth hostel, and the closest pub to Europe. Stuart said, "Go try the First and Last, if they've got a place I'll pay for your digs." What a fantastic way to start the trip, on the generosity of an individual. He paid £50 for us to stay in the hostel, on our first night. He gave us a meal at his pub and came to the hostel first thing to pay before we set off.

We started picking up all the cigarette butts in Dover but if we'd just focussed on them, we wouldn't have left the town. I was a smoker, and I estimated I've thrown away about 10,000 butts. You see the photos after festivals, it's nuts. It's saddening. It comes from us. We spoke at schools, telling them about plastic pollution.

Photograph: Susan Pilcher

EVERYWHERE MEANS SOMETHING TO SOMEONE

RUSSELL GARDENS

I remember taking my brother and sister-in-law down for the day from Croydon to Russell Gardens. We had my lovely dog Shadow with us. Perhaps he shouldn't have been off lead, but he was. The stream was empty for some reason, and there was just a thick mud at the bottom. After a previous experience, I should have known what was going to happen. We were just strolling along taking in the air, when we heard a great sloppy thud to our left. The dog had jumped in, not realising that it was just mud. Or maybe he did know... He looked quite surprised though. It took some time to get him fit to be put in the car for the journey home, particularly as we had taken my brother's car.

In July this year, I finally scattered his ashes near the plaque of the massacre. I always go to sit on that bench, and the final time I took the dog there, when I knew his time was near, he spent some time trying to get into the water on a tiny low stone footbridge across the stream. That's where I scattered his ashes.

I will go back one day, but perhaps not until I have another dog. RIP Shadow.

Photograph: Susan Pilcher

EVERYWHERE MEANS SOMETHING TO SOMEONE

Dover is a place formed through specific activities. It developed because of a combination of mercantile and defensive requirements; no one thought they were adding to Dover's heritage when they were building, because they just needed to build. They weren't building structures as future heritage, and the place is essentially not nostalgic, but the port just continues to do what the port needs to do. Its decisions can be debatable, but in a way that sort of what's always happened. I think what's really interesting is that there's an active industry that is continuing to shape the town. I went to a conference in Ostend, and I was the only person to talk about a place that was still actively developing. Everyone else was saying, "What do we do with our port heritage?" I was saying our port heritage was constantly under reconstruction, and that's really interesting, being a place that is determined by that. And there's a certain kind of amazingness about that: you go up on the cliffs and watch the arrival of billions of pounds of stuff from all around the world, and the ceaseless churn of roll on, roll off ferries, and it's amazing — an incredible, logistical choreographic experience.

Photograph: Susan Pilcher

EVERYWHERE MEANS SOMETHING TO SOMEONE

Have you ever fancied trying your hand at bowls? Dover Bowling Club has been active since 1907, with barely an interruption, except for an unexploded wartime shell on the green. There's no age limit, and even local primary schools use the green. The club has lots of facilities and on the first Saturday in May we have a free Open Day, where advice and equipment is on hand and people can have a go. Most of our members live in Dover, some come from further afield, and we have a bar and great facilities in our well-equipped clubhouse. Most of our members are active bowlers, but we do have social members too, who just enjoy being part of club activities. We have friendly games with other clubs and are part of the Kent County Bowling Association. You can call us on 07526 706804 to find out more; just leave a message and we'll get back.

....

It was a special moment when I first came across the Bowling Green in the middle of Dover. At the back of Kent College, from the Bus Station you walk up along the Dour towards the Maison Dieu, and just before you get there you come across this lawn, with this tiny little club house. It's kept immaculate, it's like there's not a weed in the lawn, it's manicured, and it manages it in the middle of Dover. Bowling Greens are always like that; you can't believe that it's actual grass. I've haven't seen a game being played, but that so often happens; when you think that there is nothing going on in Dover, there's loads going on.

Photograph: Rebecca Sperini

EVERYWHERE MEANS SOMETHING TO SOMEONE

The Eagle is a pub on London Road, it's the big whitish greyish red pub. My mum told me that it was once an execution place in the olden days. I don't know when they stopped doing it. People were, like, held there like a prison, and I think it was like hanging and stuff for criminals. It's dark. I don't know much though, but I think about that every time I go past it. Dark!

Photograph: Susan Pilcher

EVERYWHERE MEANS SOMETHING TO SOMEONE

WELLINGTON DOCK

My mum worked in the office of the ship building yard. There's still a company there that repairs little boats, but the Wellington Dock used to have all these ships coming in. You had these shipwrights who could fix them, make rope, and all these other things. Dover had quite a massive industry around there. As the ships that needed repairing got fewer and fewer, so the need for these skills decreased. Sharp and Enright's ships' chandlers is still going, but it's mostly the little boats and yachts that need fixing now.

....

There's a new lock that leads into Wellington Dock. There's a measuring stick at the end, and you can see how deep the water level is when the tide is up.

Photograph: Strange Cargo

EVERYWHERE MEANS SOMETHING TO SOMEONE

Pencester is a bit of everything. It's a park, it's a bus station, it's a hangout area, it's got all sorts of people, it has a skatepark and a graveyard. It's pretty much everything but a garden. If you call it Pencester Gardens, you're posh.

When you say, "Lets meet at Pencester," it could mean so many things: it could be the carpark end, the skatepark, the walkway towards 'Spoons, it's weirdly central.

I only really go to the skatepark.

When I was little in the park, I played tag with my mate. I was just at the park with my mum, and he was just at the park with his mum. We were playing and then we started playing together, playing tag. Our mums became friends and we're all still friends now and hang out.

Photograph: Rebecca Sperini

EVERYWHERE MEANS SOMETHING TO SOMEONE

I worked in the building with the bear on the front, it was Principals back then. The bear statue stands on the plinth on the front of the building at 42 Biggin Street. Way back, the bear building was the original Marks and Spencer shop. It's a local landmark. It was originally a barber's bear — everyone knows it. Everyone feels it had to have been a barber's bear, as apparently it originally had a pole it was holding onto.

....

We've got the huge polar bear in the museum. Everyone knows about our polar bear. There are plans to move it back to Maison Dieu when the refurbishment is all done.

....

Dover's military history is what brought me here in 1988. I was brought in as part of a team of three to move Dover Museum from Ladywell underneath the Town Hall, to a new site as part of the White Cliffs Experience, which is what the range of buildings around the Museum were originally built for. Every Dovorian remembers the big polar bear, some with fondness, some with trepidation.

....

The polar bear's enormousness was overwhelming as a child when I first saw it.

Photograph: Strange Cargo

Ray Warner filmed Dover events for years and his son Chris gave all the films to the Dover Museum. I'm working through all his films, and we show them at Dover Film Festival at the cinema in the museum every year. This year we showed 1983.

When the Borough of Dover changed to the District Council, they funded Ray to widen the events filming to outside Dover, like Sandwich and Deal. One of the things he filmed was grapes being picked and processed into the wine and then tasting the wine. We're going to show his film and, in the interval, do a bit of wine tasting.

Now the local wines are made under the name Barnsole. We will taste four wines for £2 and a draw will be made by the Mayor for three prizes. The money raised is to fund entertainment in Market Square.

Photograph: Susan Pilcher

EVERYWHERE MEANS SOMETHING TO SOMEONE

ELMS VALE RECREATION GROUND

I live in Elms Vale Way with my terrier, Holly. There's a little cross in the woods at Elms Vale recreation ground — someone's whose dog was called Paris, a Chihuahua, has put it there, with a photo of her and her collar, and it says 'This was Paris's favourite walk, as you go past this say hello to her'.

Elms Vale Rec is a big dog walking area. Six benches have been installed for dog walkers, who started meeting up in the pandemic and had nowhere to sit. So they'd walk their hounds, several of whom have died sadly, but they sit on the benches and think about them. The benches are at the far end of the rec, so they are not near the pitches where the dogs might decide to join in the football. They're not just wooden ones, they're wrought iron with pictures on.

I don't know if the name is unique to Dover, but we call these big flying bugs, a bit like a large flying beetle, July bugs. When we were kids we used to carry tennis racquets with us across Elms Vale Rec as the air was black with them. We'd have our hoods up and run like crazy, as I'd always been told they would nest in your hair, which I thought was terrifying. We'd go out for a run with the dog, and I always kept my hood up — and they were so noisy when they fly close to your ears.

Photograph: Rebecca Sperini

The idea is to build a sort of digital centre for South Kent College to run. A lot of towns have a university and it helps the economy, so hopefully having the Beacon and, from my point of view, being able to go and see young people and get help with websites and social media, will be a good thing. I have spoken to the college, and I will be able to go and chat with the media students at the college about my work, hopefully they will get something out of meeting me, and I will get something out of meeting them.

One of the things that I think would be really great, if we could have a bridge that went over Townwall Street, because a lot of people don't like going down the underpass. I would like to have 22 steps going up and 22 steps going back down. There are 43 Dovers worldwide, mainly in America — you've heard of Dover, Delaware, Dover, Jamaica… there are 43, and the 44th one is Dover itself: Dover, UK. The idea is each one of those steps would have a Dover on with some information about them. From a point of tourism this would be very interesting.

Photograph: Susan Pilcher

EVERYWHERE MEANS SOMETHING TO SOMEONE

I'm a photographer — I mainly photograph birds, it saves putting the heating on in the house. I took a photo of a Turnstone bird, you see it going along the shoreline turning all the stones. I saw this one looking for loose change on Swimmers' Beach.

Photograph: David Todd

EVERYWHERE MEANS SOMETHING TO SOMEONE

We used to do a sponsored walk in September, and the whole school would all go to Sandwich and make their way back to Dover College. There was a mapped-out route, and I was always at the halfway point, checking people in and out at the Rutland Arms on Kingsdown Beach.

We packed up there and, as far as we were aware, everyone had come through and were well on their way back to school, so I went back to school to check-in all the staff and pupils, but we'd lost one girl! We couldn't find her, couldn't get hold of her on her mobile, had no idea where she was. It turned out she didn't want to walk with the others and had deviated from the route, thought she'd follow the road and ended up walking part way down Jubilee Way and across the cliffs above Dover. Everyone else had already arrived back at school and when we finally managed to get hold of her, when we had a signal, we couldn't understand where she was at all and had to guide her by landmarks to a place where we could pick her up.

Photograph: Susan Pilcher

EVERYWHERE MEANS SOMETHING TO SOMEONE

Last year, just before I went away for Christmas, I spotted a little leaf warbler. They just catch your eye, flying about quickly, but trying to capture a photo of one is difficult. It was a Hume's leaf warbler — normally they land over at St Margaret's in the ponds. This river, the Dour, is a little attraction for these sort of things.

Photograph: Susan Pilcher

I know this is on the outskirts of Dover town, but every year for my father-in-law's birthday, we take him to the Lord of Lydden motorcycle race and side car burn up!

I had never been to see motorcycle racing before; the first time I went I wore my old motorcycle jacket from my punk gig days, assuming that's what everyone would be wearing. I was the only one. Everyone who wasn't a racer was wearing sensible hiking waterproofs and warm clothes. Having only ever ridden a motorbike once, around a friend's field years ago, I couldn't help feeling like a bit of a fraud. The rest of the day was amazing though. You got to see lots of different classes of bikes, sidecars and scooters race and everything had exciting 'metal' names, like the Devil's Elbow, which was the corner where lots of people fell off.

Photograph: Richie Moment

Swimmers' Beach is sort of Channel swimmer central. It's the bit of beach to the left of the slipway as you look out to sea. And generally, pretty much every morning, unless the weather's truly bad, you'll get people on their own, who've swum right through their lives here, dipping in the harbour. Then there's the training season, in the run up to the Channel swimming season, which runs from May through to September, October time.

There was, funnily enough, a relay swim last weekend — astonishingly, as it's February. 14 hours — the boys' team finished, the girls' didn't. Not because they couldn't swim it, but their boat had a failure. It was heartbreaking, but it was quite out of season to do it. They'd usually do it when the weather and light was better. But yes, Swimmers' Beach is called that as its traditionally where people get in and swim. There's usually plenty of people with dry robes sitting round. There's the Dover Darlings and the Kings Swimmers. And don't forget to visit the White Horse to see the names of all the Channel swimmers on the walls, but I am sure you've already been told about that.

Photograph: Susan Pilcher

EVERYWHERE MEANS SOMETHING TO SOMEONE

We arrived on Saturday afternoon and stayed until early Sunday morning with the Thanet Ghost Watch team — about 30 odd people, a mix of sceptics and believers. They had sound equipment and set up talcum powder and marbles to watch for movement. We had time on each level and then met as a group in the Council Chamber to report back.

Whilst in the Chamber they watched for orbs on their devices, which is a spiritual ball of light. Some were seen where I'm sat now. A large orb came straight through the open door and down under where I was sitting. You can't see it with the human eye, but the team could see it through their devices.

There was a young girl called Lizzie, she was one of the former maids in this building. I only found out later that all the time she was sat beside me. On the night itself, we found about six spirits. I used to sense things. Even the Mayor used to say she was aware of something moving in the Council Chamber, because of course the building's not changed, and spirits move as they would have in their lifetime, because the top floor is where they would have slept.

Photograph: Strange Cargo

EVERYWHERE MEANS SOMETHING TO SOMEONE

On Whinless Down we found lots of Stone Age and Bronze Age struck flints. It's likely it was like a prehistoric flint factory. It's steep and is easy to dig into the bank there to collect fresh flint to make tools.

You can see some shaped slightly to make a scraper, and the flat part is where they've hit it off another bit of flint, and you get what's called a point of percussion; then you get the bulbar percussion, and you only get that on flint that's been worked by people to make things. Little nibbles round the edge make it sharper, so someone might have used it to scrape a skin for making clothes, or for cutting things. The features show you they were struck by humans and not caused by the weather. Sometimes you find that they have a little point on them that was used for making holes through leather pelts, so they could be sewn together. They're like the Bronze and Stone Age Swiss Army knife. You'll find them scattered all around the bottom of hills in Dover because they wash down. Most are struck flints, struck off the core, but some have nibbling done to make serrated edges, or a long blade.

Photograph: Strange Cargo

The Roundhouse Theatre was an ideal performance space, as it was purpose-built as a theatre. It was a focal point for the town. It was so popular, it was difficult to get into there without a great deal of pushing.

There was a campaign to stop it closing. They've relocated the library out of the Dover Discovery Centre. If you just have a look at the back, it's literally round.

We did loads of plays there, and we created new work there too. Daniel, one of our ex-students, who is also on the committee at the moment, has written and created loads of work for us, and we're combining classics for production, like *New Stockings* by Jessica Swale with things like *Gamblers* by Michael Thomas, which is new.

Photograph: Susan Pilcher

EVERYWHERE MEANS SOMETHING TO SOMEONE

I manage the local community centre and I love that. It's my community, it's where I live. I watched it being built and took my kids to stuff there, and then it was unloved for a number of years. It's a massive blue and red building. I took over at a time when it was about as near to closure as it could possibly be. Now we're five years in, and it's financially viable and the building's fit, and the next step is to get the community back in. I'd like to see everyone who I can see when I stand at the front door come and use it.

There are exercise classes. We have an active coffee morning on a Thursday, and when kids are off school, locals organise odd events and every now and then they'll have a quiz, or an American supper, and we give them the hall. We have multi-generational local people and families, and people come in the school holidays — then there's everyone from nought to 85.

We've started an older youth club once a fortnight, and there's a pool table and a Nintendo Switch, and they can connect their phones. A couple of local teachers volunteer for it.

Photograph: Strange Cargo

Dover Youth Theatre did *Peter Pan* in Pencester Gardens, with two flight rigs. Commemoration stamps were made of the whole thing. It was a live broadcast by BBC Radio Kent — that was in 2002.

We had newly-composed music by the Dover Grammar Girls' Orchestra, so we involved lots of other people. There was a real community around it.

Peter Pan was probably the most difficult play. You have children flying in the open air. Vivienne and I were literally on the ground holding ropes so the kids wouldn't fall from the flight rigs. They trained for eight weeks. We went over to train with Expressive Feet and the Kent Circus School. It's not just about acting, it's about other performance skills, it's a very creative process.

Photograph: Hannah Prizeman

DOVER KENT
C
20. AU 02
Post
Office

20. AU 02
Post
Office

20. AU 02
Post
Office

**Dover Youth Theatre chose PETER PAN
for their special Summer 2002 presentation**

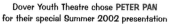

Peter

The Pirates

The Company

The Darlings

Hook threatens Peter

I play drums and piano. I play in youth church bands, including one at Salem Baptist Church. It's a very good church. I've not played, like, gigs at that church though, but I've played at One Church, up at Tower Hamlets. That's where I play, on the second Sunday of the month. It depends how many youth people come, but sometimes you can play to a few people and it's really fun.

There's different instruments in the band, like bass and piano and drums. I've done it for three months now and I'm going to play more. We play worship songs; it depends on what people want to play really.

I like it there because it's a really big building and you can do so many activities there. I'm 12 and I'll be 13 soon. To be in the band you need to be in Year 8, but then Year 6 and older come to that group as well.

Photograph: Mary Glow

MOATS BULWARK

No one ever notices Moats Bulwark. It's quite overgrown, but when you look there are all these bricks and steps on the cliff. I think it was Henry VIII who wanted to protect the newly-expanded harbour, and restock his ships, so there are tunnels in the cliff that you can just about see on a good day, where little carts would fill up at the Castle and then be wheeled down to this landing stage —16th century, I think it is. It's old bricks, but what got me was the ships would literally sail up to it, it was a quay, and they'd load it all up with supplies. I used to think it would make an gorgeous tearoom, but of course it's the other side of the A20 in the undergrowth; 14 million people go past and don't even know it's there. Park on the seafront, and you'll see it.

Bulwark means wharf. Anything they needed from the Castle would be delivered up there, it literally went down in the little carts, down to the ship and they'd sail away.

....

The 'bulwark subtus castrum Doveri' was probably built in 1539, when the French Ambassador saw 'the new ramparts and bulwarks in the rock where the sea beats'.

Photograph: Mary Glow

EVERYWHERE MEANS SOMETHING TO SOMEONE

My mum and dad lived just around the corner. I can't remember the name of it — Stembrook! They had a one up, one down. I wasn't born then, but they got shelled out and put to Elvington to live, they had a lovely house there.

My brother was 11 at the time, he had to go to Wales to live. He didn't like it. He's 95 next month, he's still around. He used to go to the school, him and his wife, and tell the children all about the war. He's called John Smith, it's an unusual name. He's on Lewisham Road now.

Because my mum was shelled out, I was born in Elvington, the miners' village. My dad was a miner, he spent 50 years down the mines. My mum and dad lived on Stembrook at number three, and their parents lived at number 16. Shelled out and then to Elvington.

Photograph: Susan Pilcher

My family lived at Dover Castle. I had a big scare with my girlfriend when we were going up there once. At the top of the stairs, you turn into the Castle and there was a big mirror on the wall, and the car headlights coming up the road reflected in the mirror and into the guard room. Anyway, we came up and looked in this mirror and you could see this pair of eyes looking at you. And my girlfriend said, "What's that?" and I went, "I don't know," well, I probably said, "You go first and have a look." We stood there for a minute, thinking there's something wrong here. But then we worked out what it was — you had the mirror, you had the light in the guard room, and you had a puddle. The light in the guard room was reflecting into the puddle and into the mirror, and all you can see was these slits. We were relieved when we realised what it was.

The regiment used to do a three year turn, then go to live somewhere else, but we were there all the time. It was great, absolutely fantastic, I'd live there now if I could.

Photograph: Amy West

Have people told you about the Western Heights? It's like a big fortress on the west side that is sunken into the hillside. There's over four miles of sunken defensive ditches. The first earthworks were started up the west end in the 1790s, with the American Wars of Independence. The French and the Dutch sided with the rebels in America and they thought there was going to be an invasion, so they started building earthworks, but then stopped when the threat died down. Then, when Napoleon was threatening in 1804, they started works again around the Grand Shaft area.

They started building things in the Drop Redoubt in about 1804 and then, with the Battle of Waterloo, they stopped. In the 1850s and 1860s there was the threat of war with France which started building once again; it was on and off throughout the 19th century.

At the White Cliffs Countryside Project, we manage all the green areas around the town as a nature reserve, and English Heritage owns the Drop Redoubt in certain areas. The Home Office did own the Citadel, which was the big fortress, but now it's Techfort that owns that. I think they're planning to turn it into a business innovation centre.

Photograph: Amy West

You know when we had the hurricane in 1987? Well apparently there was another one back in 1703, when lots of people died, and I think it was back then that the mouth of the river Dour got diverted by a shingle bank which was thrown up by the weather. The river now goes round and out through Wellington Dock, so the hurricane changed the mouth of the river Dour and made it flow in a different direction.

The Dour turns at Townwall Street and does a bit of a right hand turn past where De Bradelei Wharf is and into Wellington Dock and Granville Dock. After the 1703 hurricane, the river started silting up. Before that, in medieval times, the pilgrims and all the people who were travelling could get on a boat at the Town Hall, at Maison Dieu — the river was navigable until that point, and they could get on boats there.

Apparently when the Crusaders were stopping off before they went on to Jerusalem, they would stay at Maison Dieu and then sail from there, so it's changed a lot in a thousand years.

Photograph: Susan Pilcher

EVERYWHERE MEANS SOMETHING TO SOMEONE

The exciting thing is that the Kent Downs and the chalky areas on the other side of the Channel in France used to all be one geological unit, an anticline of chalk and different rocks.

About 50 million years ago, when the African continent drifted north and hit the European continent and caused lots of crumpling and geological uplift which formed the Alps, it crumpled up the south of England and our strata, which was flat then, got bunched up into a dome. Gradually that's been eroded off, and when you look at a geological map which shows the North and South Downs and the sides that were connected, you can see the top's been scoured off by the weather. That anticline structure, that dome, went across the Channel and goes into France, and we're all connected by the same geology. If the aspiring Geo Park UNESCO bid is successful, which I hope it will be, the undersea geology will be included as part of the Geo Park, and it will be the first programme that includes the undersea geology in the world.

Photograph: Susan Pilcher

EVERYWHERE MEANS SOMETHING TO SOMEONE

Tom Casey was a brilliant bloke; he's gone now. He told me that, as a lad during the war, he was an apprentice boiler smith at a packet yard in Dover. They were commissioned to service a boiler on a trawler which had a steam mortar on it, which worked on the principle of using high pressure steam to fire projectiles. When all the men went off to the pub for lunch, they left the two young apprentices on board and, whilst unsupervised, they decided to try out the steam mortar.

They went to the galley and found some vegetables, and they shot turnips out of the steam mortar, at full velocity, straight through a dinghy moored in the harbour, sinking it! The dinghy apparently belonged to the Harbour Master. Tom got into lots of trouble. I think he got dismissed, but was then reinstated without pay because of the manpower shortage during the war, and he had to rebuild the dinghy to compensate.

I made the sculpture on top of the pagoda at Cullins Yard to commemorate this as Tom, the turnips, and the Harbour Master's boat, is such a great story.

Photograph: Strange Cargo

EVERYWHERE MEANS SOMETHING TO SOMEONE

Right at the top of Maison Dieu there are these little, ornamental carved grotesques (that's gargoyles without the waterspout) — dragons and griffins, all along the top edge. They're very weathered. Some are Victorian additions by William Burgess; some of his were replaced in the 1930s because they were in poor condition; and there are some medieval ones. It's just layer upon layer of history here. There are Victorian cells where inmates were washed, with all these fabulous carvings over the entrances for different types of prisoners: Vagrants, Debtors, Felony For Trial.

There is a medieval tomb in what was originally part of the medieval stone hall of the Pilgrim's Hospital. It was when they installed the prison in the Victorian period that they raised the floor by an entire storey. In the 1920s they knocked through the prison wall and rediscovered the tomb recess. They found some bone fragments there and some decorated fragments of medieval tiles, but the coffin lid isn't original; it was discovered when they built the Connaught Hall, and that was a convenient place to put it.

Photograph: Alex Davies

Do you remember there was a dance hall in Castle Street? It was a big one. It got knocked down and became a nightclub. I'm sure it was a ballroom as well.

You know where the Heart Foundation is on Castle Street? It was right next to that.

My son used to do the chips down there, he used to do the drying and used to dress up smart. The Granada Hall, they used to have live shows there, and singers.

It came down maybe 1997, the landlords sold it and it was knocked down, it's still a derelict site.

Photograph: Susan Pilcher

EVERYWHERE MEANS SOMETHING TO SOMEONE

We both went to secondary school at Astor and we met through starting work at Dover Charlton Centre, 35 odd years ago. This is the actual High Street up here, some people don't realise that. A lot of people shop here.

Our shop will have been here five years in June, and we've started stocking much more crafting stuff, as it's becoming far more popular. Crochet has really taken off, it's the big thing really. I love crocheting, it's something we've learned to do since we've been running the shop, as we've got someone who comes in and does classes, which has taught us a lot too. We are the only craft shop in town. We were both made redundant from our previous jobs, and it only took us 12 weeks to get up and running. We sell all the yarns, fabrics, and crafty bits, but obviously, Big Local do a craft day, especially during the holidays, and if there's anything they need we try and get it in. Crochet and knitting are really good for your mental health, especially if you suffer from anxiety. We've had lots of regulars who've told us how much it helps them.

Photograph: Susan Pilcher

I've photographed two rare birds here.

Five years ago, I was stood on the green bridge in Pencester Gardens with a new little camera. It was the middle of February and this thing popped out of a tree, caught a fly and went back in. It was tiny and I thought, that doesn't happen this time of year.

So, I managed to wait for the next time it popped out the tree to catch a fly and I caught a photo of it on the branch and I just put it on a Kent Birds website. Someone said, "Dave, do you know what that is?" And I said, "No," I wasn't really into birds as much then. He said, "It's a Yellow-Browed Warbler." I said, "What's one of them?" They're pretty rare... I mean I *say* they're rare, but they're only rare because they're not seen or recorded. They're just coming through, they shouldn't be here, they should be in India somewhere.

I got one last year, and about 300 came from all over to see it. I was taking them to La Salle Verte café, spending all my grandkids' money.

Photograph: David Todd

EVERYWHERE MEANS SOMETHING TO SOMEONE

In 2007 someone I knew, who was in his early 20s at the time, went up onto the cliff to a favourite lookout spot over Dover Marina. It's about 100ft above the road below, and it's where he would often go to hang out with friends.

On this occasion he was there on his own after dark and was a bit tipsy and, when he went to stand up, he missed his footing and fell backwards off the cliff! Fortunately, as he fell, he became entangled in some large shrubs growing out of the chalk face which were strong enough to hold his weight. He was still conscious and hadn't broken any bones, but no one heard his cries for help. Thankfully, he still had his mobile phone in his pocket — he had one of those old mobiles that could give out an SOS signal, or flashing beacon or something of that nature. Whatever it was, it meant the emergency services knew he was in trouble and could pinpoint his location — this was back before everyone had a smartphone. He was eventually rescued by helicopter, or someone abseiling down to get him, I can't quite remember how. When I saw him the following day, I couldn't believe his lucky escape as he got away with only a few scratches.

Photograph: Rebecca Sperini

As far as we know, it's been here since the Second World War. We've lived here since 2016, and when we arrived it was just filled to the brim with rubbish — there was rubble, bits of bathroom, polystyrene, it was full to the top. I thought it was such a shame, as it's such a piece of history. The person who owned it before us used to have two green doors on it and stored their motorbike inside: what a good idea!

Someone said to me, "What if there's a tunnel that goes all the way back through the garden behind it?!" — and my children now think that's what's there. There's something written on the corrugated wall inside. It's a stencilled image of a fountain and the letters HO, apparently when you look online this is the manufacturers' marks stamped on the metal by companies authorised by the Home Office ('HO') to supply sheets of corrugated iron for Anderson shelters.

There was a chat on Facebook and someone said that apparently there are several Anderson shelters left around Dover, a few in allotments, and one that's in a cellar.

Photograph: Strange Cargo

A small thing, but indelibly etched on my mind in the 1970s: As holidaying students from the north, we always visited the Cinque Port Arms on the Western Docks, before catching the ferry into Europe. It was handily placed near the terminal. We drank fizzy, tasteless Double Diamond beer and ordered slightly dodgy-looking pickled eggs from a large jar on the bar. It all set us up nicely for the frequently choppy crossing on the Sealink Ferry. Great days!

....

I love the Cinque Port Arms as it's a little off the beaten track and it feels like the area has its own vibe. It's a 17th century pub with lots of history. Located close to the Western Docks cruise terminal, and a ten minute walk to town. It has a really friendly atmosphere and staff, free wi-fi, and serves a full range of beers, ciders, and hot drinks. There's a beer garden and a pool table and darts too. It is dog friendly and has nice rooms available if you fancy staying over. What more could you want from pub?

Photograph: Susan Pilcher

A lot of Dover locals have memories of Biggin Hall from when they were younger. Using it as a wedding party venue… Emma who I work with, her nan, there's a photo of her here in the 50s.

It's also been the baths, and it was also something else. It was built in 1881, there's a lot of really good Dover history here. People frickin' love Dover history. So, the baths are still here, you just open up that hatch in the floor and they're underneath.

Yeah, I think they were built due to health problems and the lack of bathing facilities in Dover homes, so you'd just come here for a bath.

I've seen it down there, under the floorboards, it's really dark and gloomy. There's little steps down there; I poked my head down and from what you can see the baths are tiled and it looks like a lot of concrete. You can see marks up here where all of the different baths are placed and there's these holes in the floorboards above each bath — I think for ventilation.

Photograph: Rebecca Sperini

We used to have a Boys' Brigade near here at St Martin's Church; it's like a semi-religious sort of Scouts thing. Every year we'd go away for two weeks' holiday, we'd go camping. They'd throw all the tents and everything on a lorry, then you'd have another lorry with lots of stuff on it, and then when everything was on there, Reverend Galpin would say, "Right lads, get on," and we'd all get on the back of these lorries — an open-backed lorry, with 30 - 40 kids hanging on around all these tents and things.

When we were camping, we had to go into a little village to get some jam and stuff. Anyway, on the way back there was a barbed wire fence. The guy I was with lifted the barbed wire for me to go through, but he let it go — he didn't do it on purpose, but it cut me right across the forehead. It wasn't a deep cut, but it was a big, long cut, blood all over the place, so I go back to the camp and Reverend Galpin was there and he said, "Let's have a look at that. Oh, we'll put some yellow muck on that!" Of course, that was iodine. You could break your leg and he would have put some yellow muck on it.

If that had happened today, I would have been in A&E. There would have been an ambulance up there. In those days, it was just bliss, it really was.

Photograph: Susan Pilcher

EVERYWHERE MEANS SOMETHING TO SOMEONE

Psalm 23

The Lord is my shepherd, I lack nothing.

He makes me lie down in green pastures,
He leads me beside quiet waters,
He refreshes my soul.

He guides me along the right paths for
His name's sake.

Even though I walk through the darkest valley,
I will fear no evil, for You are with me,
Your rod and your staff, they comfort me.

You prepare a table before me in the presence of
my enemies. You anoint my head with oil,
my cup overflows.

Surely your goodness and love will follow me all
the days of my life, and I will dwell in the house
of the Lord forever.

Dover feels like a place grassroots activity can happen. You wouldn't think there are a lot of community connections, but there actually are. People do kind of talk to each other and support each other here, perhaps more than in a gentrified area. People are really willing to talk to you. All of the shops want things to happen here. Dover Pride is a great example — it starts at Biggin Hall and walks down Biggin Street, and the shops show support through their window displays.

There has been a lack of LGBT visibility in Dover, and that's why Dover Pride is so important. I don't know if you've seen it, but on Channel 4 and on Netflix, *Drag SOS* did a whole episode on Dover. Shaun Dawson is on it, he's a drag dad and also does lots of work with Dover Pride and the community.

....

I have only lived in Dover for 18 months but love it — I'm biased, because they're my friends and I'm involved, but Dover Pride and Anxious Pickle Club have made Dover home for me. I only know the recent history... but summer to me is all about Biggin Hall and Shakespeare Beach.

Photograph: Mike McFarnell

On the seabed below Langdon Cliffs, before the Bronze Age boat was unearthed in 1992, a horde of Bronze Age artefacts was discovered on the oldest known shipwreck site in British waters.

The boat wasn't there, but the cargo was, and the Sub-Aqua Club was excavating it and collecting the artefacts. When the 1987 hurricane hit it messed up their grid system, but they had collected most of the bronzes by then and sent them to the British Museum. The bronze type was analysed as that of Continental bronze, not British bronze; it was a trading vessel. The interesting thing was it was all broken artefacts, so this Bronze Age person was collecting scrap bronze from the Continent to bring back and melt down to create new items, a bit of a Bronze Age Steptoe and Son. So, it was different to the bronze being created here from Cornish copper — they analysed the chemical composition and saw that it was different and came from somewhere else. Some of the artefacts from the site are on display in Dover Museum.

Photograph: Strange Cargo

If you look closely at the outside walls of Biggin Hall, you can find a really unusual architectural technique called galleting, where thin, sharp slivers of flint are pushed into the mortar around the larger pieces of knapped flint, with the edges jutting out dangerously from the wall.

Apparently, in England, galleting can be found almost exclusively in the South East between the North and South Downs, and flint was the first material to be mined in Britain around 6000BC.

We wondered if this was a defensive technique, as the hall was originally built as part of the police station, or whether the sharp shards were designed to protect the mortar from the weather. But there are also studies that suggest these sharp flint additions were imbued with a superstitious belief, aimed at warding off malevolent forces such as witches and other nefarious influences.

Photograph: Strange Cargo

EVERYWHERE MEANS SOMETHING TO SOMEONE

My nan and grandad had a pub in Dover called the Mogul. They stopped running it sometime in the early 2000s.

They lived above it and had a lot of regulars there, they met some real characters. My grandad, he used to be in the Navy, so they had a lot of ship workers, boat workers come into the pub. It was like the ship workers' pub. Sailors are so tough.

There's also a super old graveyard at the back of the pub, which isn't in use anymore. I wonder if it was a sailors' graveyard. I was a bit scared of it when I was younger. I didn't really spend time in it, but my grandad told me lots of stories about it in later years. There's a hidden tomb in there, there's so much underground in Dover, I guess with the smuggling history and the tunnels leading up to the Castle.

But a tomb, a boxed room, underground. I guess it depends on who that person was. I don't know, but someone's buried there with their possessions.

Photograph: Rebecca Sperini

I was always sports-mad as a child so every weekend, especially in the winter, my mum would take me to the old sports centre on Townwall Street to let off steam. I would swim, play squash, badminton, and table tennis.

I think though the most exciting part of the trip was deciding what delight to get from the vending machine... hot chocolate? Soup? The possibilities seemed endless at that young age. The drinks would come out the temperature of molten lava, so you could taste the plastic cup too — mmm.

Photograph: Susan Pilcher

High on the cliffs, overlooking Dover's ferry dock, there's a site visited by thousands each year. This is the White Cliffs Centre and restaurant, owned and run by English Heritage, which has bought up much of the tops of the White Cliffs of Dover.

Few of the visitors, who come in their cars from miles around, realise the grim history of the site where they sip their coffee while watching shipping in the Dover Strait.

On this land stood a prison surrounded by high walls and a fortress-style entrance gate. The prison was originally provided to accommodate civilian prisoners destined to help build the massive Dover Harbour. Later, the prison was taken over by the military where harsh treatment awaited soldiers, who were to be thrown out of the Army following courts martial.

Still later, the prison was taken over as a civilian place of detention and, during the two wars, was used to detain enemy prisoners for a short time. After the Second World War the prison, with its high walls, was no longer wanted and was demolished. Just a few foundations remain to remind of its grim history.

Photograph: Mary Glow

EVERYWHERE MEANS SOMETHING TO SOMEONE

I grew up in Dover and I love this shelter. It's been there my whole life, and we used to play in there when I was a child. I'm 85 now.

There used to be a big, stone horse trough in front of it, which is now down at Stembrook behind St Mary's Church. I want it back here please. It always was here, because you know there used to be an abattoir up here and they used to bring the cows and horses down. They came off the meadows and all down Cow Lane, where I live now, and they used to drink there from the trough.

The shelter was painted a couple of weeks ago, and some of the glass was replaced; it does sometimes get vandalised. It's a Dover landmark, because so much is being demolished. It has never been a bus stop, just a place for people to shelter.

Photograph: Strange Cargo

My school is Dover Girls' School, and it is literally like Hogwart's in there. It's divided up into houses, and I was in the Stephen de Pencester house. I was Drama Captain for our house. Everyone used to call it Stephen, and our house colour was yellow.

It was named after Stephen de Pencester, who was Lord Warden of the Cinque Ports. He was a Navy man, around like the 1200s I think maybe.

He was high up, and there's an effigy of him somewhere, I think it's in one of the stained-glass windows at Maison Dieu. His title was Keeper of the Coast, and Pencester Gardens is named after him.

Photograph: Rebecca Sperini

There's a load of amazing architecture here. Dover developed inland into the valleys in more recent times. London Road is a sort of 1840s expansion of the town, and there are some great examples of late Georgian architecture there. Dover grew as a resort then, and a lot of the housing was built for people who would decamp from London and come to Dover to take a house for the summer. Whole families with their staff would arrive.

There was the expansion along the seafront as well, and then the development of the High Street, which is late 19th century, early 20th century. So, there were chunks of time when things happened, and things changed quite a lot; and then a lot of times when nothing happened. The other thing is just how much was damaged by bombing the town was during the war, we just lost masses of stuff.

Photograph: Susan Pilcher

THE GRAND SHAFT

It always interests me that the Grand Shaft was based on something in Orvieto in Italy, which was a Renaissance well with a trackway for mules to go down to reach the well. I don't know if Twiss, who designed the one at Dover, had seen it or not.

....

Dover Arts Development have got into some really cool abandoned forts and spaces to do exhibitions and stuff. There's somewhere called the Grand Shaft — I went to an amazing event they did there. I don't know what year the building is from, it's really strange architecture, like a spiral staircase. It was, like, a live music performance in this really historical structure.

Photograph: Susan Pilcher

EVERYWHERE MEANS SOMETHING TO SOMEONE

We bought this place just before Covid hit, and it's not a bad place to get stuck. We had all sorts of crazy things happen here. There are constantly all these weird noises happening on site. The big building at the front is the old Officers' Mess and, if you look at the plans, there's a place in the building called the 'punishment cells'. I've been down there a couple of times, and we had some guys working on site to do some clearance down there, and these two massive guys that I would never think would be frightened by anything, they were like, "David, were you down there?" They could hear a conversation between two people that sounded like it was over a radio, in the punishment cells, and when they came up and I told them I wasn't there, they told me they were carrying something out and they felt this thing coming over them, they dropped what they were carrying and came to find me — they were completely pale and they said, "We don't want to go in there anymore."

I've been in there and I've heard some weird stuff myself too.

Photograph: Strange Cargo

EVERYWHERE MEANS SOMETHING TO SOMEONE

We currently run four businesses in the market. We sell all sorts really — we do household goods, DIY, gardening plants and tools, toys... a bit of everything. Whatever you might want, you'll probably find it here. We also do party balloons and things like that. There's a shop here for recycled baby clothes and equipment, selling second-hand prams and pushchairs. Emma at Rimskey's does sweets and giftware. My friend Dave, whose business is upstairs, runs Gardeners' Cottage — it's an internet-based business where people can order garden stuff online and then collect what they've bought from here. There used to be a very good picture framer who operated from these premises, but he retired. Originally the building was built as four terraced houses, but it would have been pretty crowded. We get to know a lot of people; there's lots of people from different places live round here. I first came here when I served in Dover in the Army.

Photograph: Strange Cargo

Some of the biggest employers were Buckland Paper Mill, the iron foundry, and the mines. Walking along Bridge Street you could see the men working in the foundry and feel the heat. When I was very young there were no pit head showers, and the miners would come home on the pit buses still covered in coal dust.

The river Dour would often be polluted with strange colours from the paper mill, and washing couldn't be hung outside if the wind was blowing from the foundry as it would be covered in smut. Shakespeare Beach was popular, but only when the tide took the sewage out to sea.

Dover then was very different from today, but one constant is the parks. Connaught Park was our nearest, and we spent a lot of time there. It was much more formal then, with floral displays. I remember one display was the Teddy Bears' Picnic. There was a whalebone arch across the path leading to a lawn, and on to a pond which was filled with goldfish. The park keeper lived in the cottage by the gate. There was usually a gardener about — very useful when my little sister accidentally locked herself in the loo.

Photograph: Susan Pilcher

Dover is the only Cinque Port still left with a port. Before the Royal Navy, if the King wanted a battle fought, he'd send us lot out in our little fishing ships, and we fought off the Dutch and the Spanish and in return we got all these favours from the King. We could have whatever washed up on the beach, we didn't pay taxes on stuff, we got a good deal out of it, but that did sort of turn us into pirates. We'd go off to France pillaging and nicking stuff — terrible! So, the King created the post of the Lord Warden, who came down to live amongst us and keep us in order. It was only when Henry VIII realised we were too unruly to control that he built his own Navy and the role of the Cinque Ports as a fighting force stopped.

Famous Lord Wardens include Winston Churchill, the Queen Mother, and Wellington. The King has just appointed Admiral Sir George Zambellas GCB, DSC, ADC, DL, as the new Lord Warden and Admiral of the Cinque Ports, in succession to Lord Boyce. The ceremony will happen at Dover College. There's a stone up on the Western Heights called the Bredenstone (it's Saxon I think), which is the base stone of the lost Pharos, and the Lord Warden has always sworn their oath on that stone.

Dover Castle from the Heights, circle of Samuel Scott (1702-1777)
Photograph: Strange Cargo
(painting hangs in Maison Dieu House)

EVERYWHERE MEANS SOMETHING TO SOMEONE

DOVER CASTLE
FROM
THE HEIGHTS.

Last year we designed this temporary lighthouse for the new Marina Curve. There were pop-ups, cafés, bands playing every weekend, and it did suddenly feel like a place. There was the brewery, where you could buy a nice pint and sit in a deckchair and watch a band playing. It's important to get people to go there and realise that there's stuff happening. Once you're there it's nice; there's this lovely beach and people swim all year round. Training and sea swimming is a much bigger thing now, so it's always pretty active down there.

There's lots of hidden stuff that's hard to get into. Lord Warden Hotel has an impressive ballroom — it's incredible, a real sleeping beauty. The Grand Shaft is only occasionally open. Marine Station, before the pandemic, Dover Harbour Board had a really popular skating rink in there. Historic England did a report that said that Dover's got a lot of empty buildings — if you want to encourage cultural activity here, then make those empty buildings attractive to people who want to use them. Fort Burgoyne is huge. In another situation these buildings would be snapped up by canny developers. The historic low land value thing means architectural assets haven't yet been reinvented.

Photograph: Richie Moment

I grew up in Balfour Road. No one owned a car then, and the roadway was our playground. We played games like 'What's the time Mr Wolf?' from pavement to pavement. The only traffic was the coalman, the laundry van and Mr Hammond, who went round the town selling vegetables from a horse-drawn cart. We would go round to Barton Path with nets and jam jars to catch minnows in the river Dour. The highlight of the week was going to Saturday morning pictures at the Odeon cinema.

As children, my sister and I loved going to George Thomas, the ironmongers, in London Road with our father. It was a prototype for Ronnie Barker's *four candles* sketch. The floor was very uneven, and it had a distinctive smell. All the staff wore brown stock coats. They seemed to sell everything. Most homes had paraffin heaters, and you would take your can to Thomas's and one of the men would disappear out the back and fill it for you. Pre B&Q, tools, hardware and household goods were bought at Thomas's or one of the other ironmongers in the town. Nails and screws were sold in small cardboard boxes or by weight, no plastic in those days.

Photograph: Susan Pilcher

Up here used to be individual shops, but the landlord is trying to find a new purpose for it. We do lots of making up here as Future Foundry if we have a big public workshop or lots to do; it's a really big space. The natural light is wonderful — it has so much potential. It gets hot in the summer, and so cold in the winter. In December this was absolutely full of artists making the big builds for the lantern parade, and we worked with around 20 schools. And we can store things, like big lanterns and things like the wooden display units that we built for the Dover Youth Festival.

....

I was shopping with my mum, and someone said there's something for kids upstairs. And when I went to look, I saw Kai, and other people my age doing sewing with artists from Future Foundry, so I stayed. I actually made this bag then — I pinned these denim scraps together and then this artist helped me sew it all together. I've been coming ever since. I come to the Forge at Future Foundry every Saturday now, for like ten weeks.

Photograph: © Josh Leppenwell / Future Foundry

EVERYWHERE MEANS SOMETHING TO SOMEONE

The last Dover Pride, the heart of it was on the Roman Lawn, but everyone had to be so careful. It's like sacred grass. People couldn't damage it because there are so many ruins underneath. It's funny that the safest way to preserve them is to bury them.

There was a massive stage, loads of stalls and stuff. I remember Dover Pride starting at Biggin Hall, going down Biggin Street and to Market Square, and then ending on the Roman Lawn where the day-long celebrations took place. There was an afterparty too, it was like a huge show with loads of different acts on.

I think a key moment for me was seeing how people's confidence has grown, like with what people wear and how comfortable they feel in their own skin. They're sort of owning the streets.

Photograph: Rebecca Sperini

EVERYWHERE MEANS SOMETHING TO SOMEONE

Everyone knows about Dover Castle, but not many people know about the existence of the Western Heights. People will be able to visit the Citadel — we're going to be doing tours and will have a visitor centre, shop, DTC-G, and a café up here.

We've got about 54 buildings on site and plan to convert some of these beautiful archways to rent out. The big prison building is going to be turned into an innovation centre. It's got this beautiful atrium inside. We've got six barrack buildings built in 1891, that are really good workshop spaces, so we're looking to bring artisan arts back: carpentry, metalwork etc, and potentially for each barrack to reflect a different skill. Once everything is up and running people can come in and try their hands at the different skills, so that they can leave with something they've made. We think weekend courses would be good; we'd get caterers up here and some of the barracks could have lodges in.

When we bought the place, my lawyers said, "You know, you're the first private owners since King George III," which is very cool.

Photograph: Strange Cargo

We've been running our club in Tower Hamlets for two years; we opened at the end of the pandemic. We've got lots of locals getting involved in boxing, and it's a great way to give young people a bit of a change of direction. We're involved in the council's Inspired to Change programme and give new boxers an opportunity to focus on something positive. We've now got people coming from Folkestone, Deal and Ramsgate, as well as from Dover. There lots of clubs in England, and our boxers have opportunities to visit and compete with other clubs, do some sparring and enter club shows, that sort of thing. If people want to get involved, they can just come along for a taster session and see how they get on.

There are a couple of boxing clubs in Dover, it's becoming a very popular sport. Dover is a small town, but we've got lots of members. We had one of our guys get through to the semi-final of the Southern Counties Championships this year, and we have entered boxers in the Haringey Box Cup at Alexandra Palace, which is a massive platform for amateur boxing. You can spot where we are by our mural outside, painted by Ed Collinson.

Photograph: Strange Cargo

Whenever I visit my friend in Dover we go for a walk along Shakespeare Beach. Along the back bit, past the makeshift fishing huts, there's a load of super-heavy old granite blocks with railings poking out of them. I have no idea where they are from. I imagine they might have been removed when they developed the harbour. I think they are interesting, and look like they have always been there. Nine times out of ten you will see a hat or a scarf, or a single glove stuck on one that someone has lost on the beach. I always think it's like an 80s Brutalist architect designed a lost-and-found depository for the beach. I hope they stay, funny little accidental and hidden things like that make Dover so special.

Photograph: Richie Moment

I had a nightclub for 16 years, between 1989 and 2005, called Nu Age. The name was meant to sound sophisticated, but the locals ended up calling it UnderAge or OverAge.

Lots of people worked there over the years, and most local people would have been there at some time. At one time the local papers accused me of being indirectly responsible for all the illegitimate children in Dover, which I thought was a little unfair.

We had many DJs over the years, and a number of well-known ones too from Radio 1 and the like. There was also live music. We had Ray Lewis from the Drifters perform regularly, and plenty of other acts. On one occasion an agency phoned me up and told me they had an up-and-coming band that wanted to publicise themselves and could I offer them a booking. They were only charging £50 and made no demands, so I said yes. It was a Thursday night, and I was astounded by the number of people that came to see them, although I didn't take that much notice of what they did. Three weeks later they were No 1 in the hit parade. It was Take That!

Photograph: Strange Cargo

EVERYWHERE MEANS SOMETHING TO SOMEONE

Have you heard about the Dover Pageant? There's been a number, right up until 2005 I believe, but the one that was performed in the grounds of Dover College in 1908 really galvanised the locals into cooperative action and gripped the town.

There was a cast and chorus of 2000 people from Dover and nearby. But the Pageant was a bit loose with facts. Indeed, the laughing audience was told the performance would only describe events that 'actually took place at Dover, or ought to have done' and that they were going to show 'mighty things in the history of the town,' both mythical and real. They told a story of King Arthur and his meeting with Knights of the Round Table. He was morose because Guinevere and Lancelot have left him for love, but his followers reminded him that he'd won Dover town, 'the key of the realm.'

At the end of the pageant, 44 figures, representing different Dovers from around the world, participated in a march past. It's now thought 88 Dovers exist in different parts of the globe. Even though 57,000 people saw the 13 performances, and press opinion was highly positive, the Pageant was a colossal financial failure.

Photograph: Rebecca Sperini

EVERYWHERE MEANS SOMETHING TO SOMEONE

The imposing chalk escarpment which separates Maxton from the Elms Vale valley was known by us kids that played on it as 'Plum Pudding Hill'. An ancient trackway, Cow Lane, still climbs up its lower slopes, a reminder that livestock once grazed on the open hillside preventing the chalk grassland from becoming overrun by trees, as is sadly now the case. The dark clumps of gorse, which in earlier times dotted the grassy slopes when I was a child, were the currants of the pudding. Orchids used to grew there too.

Photograph: Strange Cargo

There was a lot of industry, for instance there was Dover Engineering Works which was a big employer. You had the gasworks, the paper mill, the Singer Sewing Machine factory — a lot of the women were employed there. We probably knew lots of women that worked there. There was also a dress factory; Lloyd's dress factory employed so many people.

....

I worked there. First we was down Finnis Hill, then Poulton Close many moons ago. About 65 years ago, when I started.

The one down Finnis Hill was pulled down when they improved Snargate Street. I think the building up Poulton Close is still there; it was the building on the left hand side as you go up Poulton Close. I am not sure when it closed, as I left when I had my son in 1970. It was not too bad, but you was not allowed to talk while you was working. We had a lady sitting behind us to make sure we didn't.

....

I remember the night it caught fire, you could see the flames up at Aycliffe, and the smell was horrendous. All gone now, for years it has been a petrol station.

Photograph: Susan Pilcher

I feel connected to the sea. There's always something happening. You can keep returning to the same place day after day and there is something different going on.

Photograph: Strange Cargo

I can remember John Angel telling me, and I remember it as a kid and others will have seen it too, there still being bomb sites that hadn't been developed. It would have been in the early 1950s, I remember walking about when they were there, still as they had been bombed.

The people of Dover wanted to have a new start, and not see the bombed buildings that were unbelievably there for ages. As you walked down onto the seafront there were bombed houses, where the Gateway flats are now.

Some of them aren't long gone. You know where we had the Banksy? That area there has only just recently had some funding. There was Caves Café which had been bombed during the war, and that was left there for years.

Photograph: Susan Pilcher

THE DUCHESS, BENCH STREET

I remember once there was a fight that broke out here, when me and my friend were in there, when it used to be called the Tavern. This nice gay chap behind the bar, he was a lovely bloke. He said, "Come on girls, come behind here, I'll look after ya," and we hid behind the bar whilst this fight went on. It's now The Duchess and I expect its less rowdy now than back in the day.

Photograph: Susan Pilcher

EVERYWHERE MEANS SOMETHING TO SOMEONE

Edith Sarah Horn was Dover born and bred. Born in 1893 at 5 Queens Court, Biggin Street, in 1901 she lived at 4 Durham Hill Cottages with her brother, parents and Grandmother Hunt. She went to Christchurch School in Military Road and her father worked from home as a tailor. She helped him with deliveries and collections. Next they moved to 48 London Road, under the name Horn. She was a mother's help. Once married she worked at the Buckland Paper Mills.

When her husband Harry James, who was a baker in Snargate Street, went to war as a machine gunner in France and was sent to a German POW camp near the River Rhine, she changed her job to a carriage cleaner at the Dover Priory Station, for SE & C Railway, so that she could look out for him. The injured men were brought home by boat and put on trains at Dover to take them to hospital. Edith's family sheltered at the Oil Mill Caves Western Docks air raid shelters.

One day the boat docked, bringing Harry back home from the POW camp. It is said that she nearly knocked several people off the gangway as she ran to him. Home at last!

Photograph: Strange Cargo

EVERYWHERE MEANS SOMETHING TO SOMEONE

Disney has its own cruise company, *Disney Magic*. During the pandemic people saw the Disney cruise ship moored in Dover for a long time. It used to go up and down along the coast to run the engines and get rid of their brown water; you would see the ferries going up and down there as well. It was bizarre time wasn't it, when the world suddenly stood still.

Our main market here is Americans and Germans, and the British market is Saga and Fred Olsen. This is where we handle the smaller ships — Saga uses it mainly, and the larger ships go in the other one, which is more like an airport.

Dover Harbour Board owns the whole estate and there's an eight-metre tidal difference when ships dock, which is taken into account when getting passengers on and off. We're a big port operation with our own equipment and we are very aware of the tides, as there's a strong current which moves a lot of shingle. We dredge a lot; our dredger is called the *David Church*. Wellington Dock has a new lock, with a 24-hour access system to get the berth holders in and out, but because of the tidal difference we make sure we always keep water in the Wellington.

Photograph: Amy West

When I was younger, I used to go out in an evening by myself; I'd go dancing at the big Town Hall. There was live music and we'd do lots of jive dancing, it was around 1957. I always felt safe in Dover, unless the Aylesham lot came over, haha … if you were friends with them, you were okay.

They used to come in on a weekend because there would be social functions going on. You'd get the Aylesham lot, the mining fraternity, and then of course you get the Navy lot coming into town and it'd get a bit volatile. But it was only ever fisty cuffs, it was never that bad. As a child in Dover… I won't name them, but there were certain families you knew the name of and you wouldn't mess with them.

Photograph: Strange Cargo

EVERYWHERE MEANS SOMETHING TO SOMEONE

Founded in 1837, the Dover Lifeboat Station has been keeping a watchful vigil over the strategically critical Straits of Dover for nearly 200 years.

With the exception of the war years of 1939-1945, the volunteer Dover Lifeboat crew has manned a number of all-weather lifeboats and occupied a number of station sites throughout the Port of Dover to provide a 24-7 all-weather offshore search and rescue capability, ultimately helping to save thousands of lives over nearly two centuries.

Finished in 2024, the current station at the end of the harbour arm is the latest station to be built and serves as a home to over 60 local volunteers, as well as our Severn Class ALB — the largest vessel in the RNLI fleet. As one of the busiest stations in the country, the Dover crew attends all manner of vessels and individuals in distress.

With a brand-new visitor centre and shop, we welcome you to visit the station!

Photograph: Susan Pilcher

If you are ever looking to lose yourself in a bit of history for a couple of hours, there's no better place to go than Dover Museum. It's guaranteed to enthral and educate you in equal measure. There are three floors, each one with a range of different galleries offering insights into the history of Dover. The beautifully constructed displays and tableaux give you the chance to escape from the outside world for a while. One of my favourites is the gallery with models which shows the evolution of the coastline. There are cabinets of curiosities, and so many unusual artefacts on display — for a small museum it has a wealth of objects. One room has changing exhibitions, which update at intervals. Its most precious treasure has its own climate-controlled room — the 3,500 Bronze Age boat which was discovered in the 1990s when the new road was constructed.

The museum is free to visit; it's all indoors, and offers the whole family something absorbing to do, especially on a rainy day. And of course, there's the famous polar bear on the landing. The staff are friendly and knowledgeable, and I wager you will find it difficult to walk out through the gift shop without buying something.

Photograph: Strange Cargo

SHAKESPEARE BEACH

Growing up in Dover was amazing. I've got such good memories. I lived down the Marina area, near Shakespeare Beach. There was our house, a railway line and then the beach — we had to cross the railway line to get to it. I was swimming in the sea at five years old; I had older siblings, so they taught me to swim. It was such a lovely area, our street had just 24 houses. Then there was the next street with 28 flats and then, just across the way, there was Victoria dwellings which were Victorian flats that had been upgraded a bit.

When my sister lived there it was just gaslight, no electricity. Simpler times. Growing up next to a beach was so special.

Photograph: Susan Pilcher

EVERYWHERE MEANS SOMETHING TO SOMEONE

I work here six days a week: it's my place. I run the café, and I do a lot with the community — I do every church, I cater for shelters, and charity events. Everyone says, if you got a problem come to Sandra. I do everything. This café is my family. I'm from Madeira, Portugal, it's a beautiful island.

Most of the people that come here think of it more like a community hub than a café. I like that. I wouldn't want to live anywhere else now. The work I do in the community brings people in here — if you are giving, people will repay the kindness back. Sometimes you can't get a table because it's so busy, but you can usually share a table with someone else, because everyone is so friendly. I've been in Dover 19 years. It's the sea, I've been drawn in because of the sea. I love the sea. I need the sea. If I'm upset, I have the sea. I'm a walker as well. Madeira, where I'm from, is famous for the Levadas, so I like the walking here.

Photograph: Rebecca Sperini

EVERYWHERE MEANS SOMETHING TO SOMEONE

When we first moved to the Citadel, I got a call from the White Cliffs people to say there's a cow that's fallen into your moat. It's a nine-metre drop. I walked all the way round twice, and I called them back and said, "There's no cow here — I'm really sure." They said, "There's definitely a cow there, we can see it." They called the fire brigade — we are about 450 feet above sea level, and these six guys carried a boat all the way up the hill, and then asked, "Where is the water, I thought you said there was a moat?"

We were told by Historic England to always call things by their proper name: it's called a *revetment*, or a dry moat, so these six poor guys carried the boat up to rescue this cow and it wasn't needed. It's a very long way up!

It ended up being a different area of the moat that we didn't know about, a sort of secret garden that we didn't realise was part of our site, it's a forgotten area of the fort that is completely overgrown and has its own ecosystem, and there was the little cow that had fallen in.

They eventually got the cow out.

Photograph: David De Min

AIR RAID SHELTER, DOVER PRIORY STATION

This Grade II listed WW2 Air Raid Patrol Warden shelter is built into the embankment as you approach Dover Priory station.

It has a blast baffle entrance, and a flat concrete roof to resist the penetration of incendiary bombs. ARP Wardens' posts were a vital part of civil defence co-ordination. Maintaining contact with other posts enabled early warning of raids to be given, and emergency assistance rendered in the case of attack to injured or trapped victims in nearby streets.

Dover had a major role in the Second World War as a military base and harbour, its proximity to the Continent and cross-Channel gunfire earning this part of Kent the unenviable title Hellfire Corner. It was from Dover Castle that the Dunkirk evacuation was directed, and the town was a major military target for enemy action. It received 464 high explosive bombs, 1,500 incendiaries, three parachute mines, three V1s and 2,226 high explosive shells fired from long-range guns in France. 216 locals were killed and several hundred injured. This shelter was one of 12 posts in wartime Dover, and is one of only two ARP posts which now survive, the other being at Pilgrims' Way. After the war it served for a time as a cabbies' shelter.

Photograph: Strange Cargo

EVERYWHERE MEANS SOMETHING TO SOMEONE

DOVER PRIORY AIR RAID PRECAUTION WAI DEN'S POST

WWII Historic Building c1939-40

National Heritage List Grade 2
Entry no. 1392469

Biggin Hall has been central to my life in Dover, but not in any of its previous uses as a Turkish bath, public toilet, or library… but as part of Dover Pride and The Anxious Pickle Club, established by icons Emma Panda and Frazer Doyle. Future Foundry runs Biggin Hall as a flexible community space to make things happen, and Pickle is a cabaret night there on a Saturday every couple of months, with rehearsals on a Monday night. It's a place to test jokes, practise lip syncs, magic tricks, hula hooping and office chair roller-skating. I'll never forget rehearsing for a Damp Disco performance in the hall, sweating in our underwear during September 2023, making up bonkers choreography to a five-song medley. Almost every Pickle show ends with Black Lace's *Superman*.

The Pickle is the ultimate you-had-to-be-there cabaret: a chaotic blur of flying by the seat of your pants hosting, showing off and in-jokes. Bats, nuns, jockeys, cherubs, gay frogs, mum dancing, bikes, fire exits, inflatable Annie Lennox sharks, confetti and fake blood. So much fake blood.

If you knew how much love went into both Dover Pride and the Pickle, you'd book off every August Bank Holiday weekend to dance and march through town. Join us!

Photograph: Emma Panda & Frazer Doyle

I saw Andrew Lloyd Webber one time at Dover Priory, but he was only passing through, and we had the late Queen Elizabeth for a Battle of Britain memorial, but that was some years ago. I know that David Bowie was photographed at the station in May 1976 when he was passing through from Paris after completing his Isolar tour.

Dover Priory was originally set up to be a temporary terminal station back in 1861, and was later upgraded as a pass-through station, when the operator was London Chatham & Dover Railway. Another fun fact was when it opened it was called Dover Town, but it was renamed Dover Priory in July 1863 after a group of adjacent monastic buildings at St Martin's Priory. The station saw much wartime traffic, including the evacuation of the children of Dover in June 1940. It was party to damage when it had the dubious honour of being the victim of the first shell to hit the town, which destroyed the passenger footbridge on 11th September 1940.

On a more recent note, Dover Priory was selected to be one of the stations that started the High-Speed service back in 2009.

Photograph: Matt Rowe

St Radigund's, a ward in Dover, figures high in the UK metrics for deprivation, but I think it's a nice place. It's a working-class suburb in a picturesque valley, 1920s-built houses surrounded by a nature reserve called Whinless Down. I got permission to paint an Op Art mural there. Ideally for murals you want a gable end or other blank wall space, and I couldn't find anything like that, but I was intrigued by this weird concrete structure in front of the Community Centre, known locally as the 'Blue Screen'. Apparently, it was built in the early 90s as an outdoor cinema and used only once. It had become sort of a vandalized no-go zone. After I'd got rid of the smashed vodka bottles and so on, I painted the whole thing this pale bluebell blue, and then painted a black, geometric Op Art image on one face. It's called 'The Ouchi Illusion', after the Japanese neuroscientist who devised it. The artwork was part of a Dover Arts Development project by artist Simon Bill.

What is Op Art? Op Art is an abbreviation of 'optical art', and the term came into regular use in the mid 1960s. It's characterised by abstract patterns, often in black and white, with a stark contrast between background and foreground.

Photograph: Simon Bill

EVERYWHERE MEANS SOMETHING TO SOMEONE

I was new here in 2018, and my barber said, "Have you been to the Western Heights?" I said, "No… What's that?" He pointed out the window: "Up there."

There is a great green hill you pass on the way into town from the station. A steep yomp through long grass and wild orchids, pinging with crickets, takes you to the dry moat of the Drop Redoubt — a huge structure, 50 foot wide and deep, hidden within the hill, so that you don't even suspect it's there. There are three of these massive underground forts. You see this moat structure first, but most of it is inside the hill, a network of tunnels and chambers (all sealed off now). The Drop Redoubt is maintained by volunteers. The Detached Bastion gives the impression of the remnants of a lost civilisation. The bigger structures have three floors (all rotted). They started building in Napoleonic times, but stopped after that war and picked it up again later in the 19th century, but it quickly became clear that there was never going to be a serious invasion from France. There are beautiful white bricks, archways and vaulted ceilings, like a cathedral. It's more beautiful and much more over-engineered than it needed to be.

Photograph: Simon Bill

EVERYWHERE MEANS SOMETHING TO SOMEONE

THE HOODEN HORSE

I think it started with May Day, and I joined the Company of Green Men. We've done wassailing at the pub car parks and the like. The Dover Hoodeners made a Hooden Horse that traditionally comes out at Christmas. He's a white horse, he's called Albinus Invictus, or Dobbin for short. Plough Sunday, which is a traditional English celebration of the beginning of the agricultural year that has seen some revival over recent years, is when the farm workers that weren't working in the winter used to do mumming plays and parade their Hooden Horses — which involves knocking at doors to ask for food and drink.

Blessing the plough ready for spring is a strong tradition, when there's a gathering of the horses and the Molly, a man in a dress, comes in and sweeps away the ashes of the old day, "Make way, make way." It's all designed for people to have a bit of fun and feel good about the place. We are also reawakening our Dover Green Man, who regularly paraded through the town up until 1842; his reappearance may be as a Babe in a Bower.

Photograph: Gilly Lucas

EVERYWHERE MEANS SOMETHING TO SOMEONE

I remember as a child passing through Dover going to the South of France with my mother, who was a young widow. It was the happiest times of my childhood. When I think back to that, her energy changed in Dover — she was a very strict English woman, but when we'd get to Dover, it was the anticipation of France, and the sea and the sun and wearing bare feet, and the change would come over her.

The South of France, where we went to meet her friend, was like these magic times. I think it laid the idea in my mind of Dover as a gateway to another world, and certainly that's how it's been for me. I absolutely love it here: the light, the views. Somebody asked me recently what I loved about Dover, and it's the views: looking out of my window I see over to the Citadel, but also to the left I can see the harbour. I can see if the M20 is running smoothly, or whether its blocked. At night the lights all along the valley look like a magical place, and out to the back I can see the Castle from the top floor. So, for me, it's the views.

Photograph: Strange Cargo

BUCKLAND PAPER MILL

Dover Arts Development's Buckland Paper Mill documentary *Watermark* is a project I am most proud of. They made Conqueror paper there, the most famous kind of paper, which was sent out across the world. The factory was running at a profit, so the workers had no idea it was going to close, and they were completely traumatised. When we decided to make the film, we took over the old Post Office and opened it as a story shop for a week. We got artefacts from the museum like dandy rolls from the factory — dandy rolls are how the watermark was made in the paper. Word got around that something's happening about the mill, and people started coming down. We got footage from this, as we had no film of the working mill and they'd pulled all the machinery out and torn the factory blocks down. It was a successful business, but there were secrets... when you watch the film you'll see that they used to let coloured water go out to the sea at night, and some people were going deaf. So nobody really knows why it closed in the end, except that it left this huge hole in Dover, and that it had been one of the last of the big industries in the town.

dadonline.uk/legacy

Photograph: Susan Pilcher

EVERYWHERE MEANS SOMETHING TO SOMEONE

For a small town there's so much hidden around every corner. For 3,500 years it's been occupied, or at least that's how old the Bronze Age boat is. If you go up to the Western Heights and look at the town, you will see it's a collection of valleys. It was a former leader of the council who actually mentioned that to me. The valleys are how Dover Town Council defines its wards, and how you can see that things are close to each other, but also separate. Go to the meadows close to Noah's Ark Road, or Tower Hamlets, which is economically in the bottom 5% in the country, but it's a close-knit community, and also in a valley. At Dover Arts Development they had a project with a German guy who took photos from high up that gives you a really good sense of how much a spine to the town the river Dour is. Because you see the river, but a lot of it is underground. Pictures from above really show you how straight and true it is, and it's worth seeing as it gives a sense of how Dover evolved.

Photograph: Susan Pilcher

I met an old soldier up at Fort Burgoyne. He told me about when he'd been stationed here, and he told me the date and it tallied with when his regiment was there. Him and his mate were sent to secure the perimeter, which was standard. He said, "We found this tunnel, and three hours later we were down at the docks. We went missing and the commanding officer sent out a search party." I thought, *okay*…, but a Major from the Royal Engineers came down and I told him the story and he said, "Yes, that makes sense." I said, "Seriously?" He told me, "It doesn't surprise me at all. There are tunnels everywhere; some of them exist and some of them are just stories."

There's one under Plum Pudding Hill which connects to somewhere or other. There's supposed to be a tunnel down from the Western Heights down to York Street, which is where they brought the French POWs down, but I don't believe that one at all, as there's no need for a tunnel, they would have marched them down the road. Probably every third or fourth person you talk to will know about a tunnel. Whether they're true or not remains to be seen.

Photograph: Susan Pilcher

EVERYWHERE MEANS SOMETHING TO SOMEONE

LORD BYRON AT DOVER

Lord Byron, who lived an infamous life of scandal, spent his final two days in Britain in Dover in 1816. He never returned. Even on his final night in London, bailiffs arrived at his house to recover debts owed to the Duchess of Devonshire. Byron arrived in Dover with friend Lord John Hobhouse, who had Byron's coach put on board ship in case the bailiffs claimed that too. They dined and lodged at The Ship on the quay, drinking light French wines. Strong winds delayed the crossing, and they spent the time walking along the White Cliffs, recalling the scene from Shakespeare's *King Lear*. After his evening meal, Byron went to St Mary's Church and paid homage to the 18th century satirist Charles Churchill, whom he had admired since he was a schoolboy. When shown his grave, Byron apparently lay down on it, and then handed the sexton looking after the church a crown to renovate it.

On the day of his sailing, he slept in late and almost missed the ship. As he sailed away, Hobhouse ran along the pier: "The dear fellow," Byron wrote, "...pulled off his cap & wav'd it to me — I gazed until I could not distinguish him any longer — God bless him for a gallant spirit and a kind one."

Lear & Cordelia, 1849-54 by Ford Madox Brown
© Tate

EVERYWHERE MEANS SOMETHING TO SOMEONE

COR. HAD YOU NOT BEEN THEIR
FATHER, THESE WHITE FLAKES
DID CHALLENGE PITY OF THEM.
WAS THIS A FACE
TO BE EXPOSED AGAINST THE
WARRING WINDS?
TO STAND AGAINST THE DEEP
DREAD BOLTED THUNDER?

MINE ENEMY'S DOG,
THOUGH HE HAD BIT ME, SHOULD
HAVE STOOD THAT NIGHT,
AGAINST MY FIRE. AND WAST THOU
FAIN, POOR FATHER,
TO HOVEL THEE WITH SWINE, AND
ROGUES FORLORN,
IN SHORT AND MUSTY STRAW.

KING LEAR.

On 31st December 1999, the streets of Dover were filled with thousands of spectators to watch the spectacle of hundreds of paper lanterns carried by local children, each lit by a flame from the Bethlehem Peace Light to celebrate the coming of a new millennium. The parade made its way to the beach where a huge crowd had gathered — an enormous sculpture, the Clock of the Second Millennium, sat on the crest of the beach. As the glowing clock, with its music and shadowy projections, chimed midnight, flames appeared, creeping across the sculpture and burning it to ashes before everyone's eyes, emitting a cascade of fireworks into the night sky.

On New Year's Day 2000, the Clock of the Third Millennium had miraculously grown out of the ashes. This fantastical, illuminated metal orrery was awaiting the arrival the Carnival of the Planets, with noisy drumbeats and extraordinary carnival costumes based on the planets of the solar system made by people from across the Dover district. As the parade arrived, the orrery whirled into action and a pyrotechnic light show spectacularly welcomed in the new Millennium to Dover. The event, by Strange Cargo, was a wonderful way to celebrate the coming of a new epoch.

Photograph: Susan Pilcher

EVERYWHERE MEANS SOMETHING TO SOMEONE

The Officers' Mess was built in 1861. At around that time the Indian Army gifted a tiger cub to the Commanding Officer, and he became the regimental pet of the 102nd Regiment of Foot, Royal Madras Fusiliers. He was called Plassey. He was named after Robert Clive's famous victory of 1757, which was also a battle honour of the Madras Fusiliers. Indeed, the cap badge of the Fusiliers depicted a tiger, a beast much respected in Indian culture for its strength, grace, and power. In 1868 the 102nd were shipped to England for the first time in 233 years, and Plassey came with them. He was documented as being well behaved on the voyage.

There exists a photo of Plassey taken on the steps of the Officers' Mess at the Citadel, and you can see the building in the photo. They would walk him around town all the time and scare the locals, but he was a pet tiger. Plassey's skull is now on display in the Global Role Gallery at the National Army Museum. Maybe one day we could have the skull back to put on display at the Citadel. We're going to name one of the hotel suites Plassey after him.

Photograph: Strange Cargo

Geological evidence shows that enormous amounts of water suddenly flowed through the English Channel, when features like hanging river valleys were cut suddenly by mega-floods. There could have been more than one, but the final one caused the land bridge between England and France to break up and fall apart. They don't know if it was the sheer weight of the water behind it, or whether it was combined with an earthquake; the Channel is on a fault line.

When it happened, billions of tons of water per second was moving through, and it might have been flooding for over three weeks — this vast amount of water just rushing down through the Channel and scouring everything as it went, with icebergs tumbling in it. Further down, it cut river valleys on both sides. What's so interesting about this is that there's not many geological mega-floods known in the world. There's one in Wyoming, but this is certainly the biggest in Europe; possibly one of the biggest in the world. And it happened on our doorstep.

Stand on the cliffs and look across to France and think about that happening. You would have seen a massive wave rolling through the Channel.

Photograph: Alan Duncan Photography
(alanduncan.com)

My grandmother, Julie Annette Green, was killed by enemy action in Dover on 13th September 1944. Ida, my mother, last saw her on to the Dover train at Cannon Street. Dover was being shelled as the train arrived and, as she stepped out of the carriage at Dover Priory, a shell exploded just outside the station. Occasionally my mother would speak about her mother's death, wondering whether she had died instantly, and if she had been alone.

In the 1970s, my brother Michael was part of a church group in Dover. He volunteered to do some work for an elderly gentleman at Tower Hamlets, who had worked for the railway and had been at Dover Priory when the shell had exploded. The Booking Hall got the full blast and, when he ran inside, he found a woman lying there. She was still alive and did not have a mark on her. He lifted her head, and she died, cradled in his arms, killed by the blast of the explosion.

My brother told the elderly man that he was the grandson of Julie Green. More than 35 years after her death, by doing a good turn to another, Michael learnt how our grandmother had died. More importantly, he could tell our mother, Ida, that her mother had died in the arms of this man.

Photograph: Strange Cargo

EVERYWHERE MEANS SOMETHING TO SOMEONE

The architect who designed St Paul's Church was the famous Augustus Welby Pugin's son, Edward W Pugin, and he designed it in the Early English style. On 15th May 1868, with the apsidal east end still incomplete, St Paul's was opened.

The church escaped serious wartime damage when, in 1940, a German shell fell nearby. But sadly, in 1987, our beautiful church was the target of an arsonist. A confessional which was being used for storage was set alight — it only took a moment for the flames to rapidly grow into an inferno, and soon it reached into the main body of the church, along the roof to the organ gallery, destroying the recently refurbished pipe organ. Though the fire brigade did its best to save the church, much damage occurred, resulting in total loss of the roof. After massive restoration, the church was re-opened 12 months later.

Two frescos painted by Henry Campbell FRSA escaped damage by the fire: *The Last Supper* and a mural in the baptistry of John the Baptist baptising Jesus over the *Herald of Free Enterprise* which sank in 1987. Several of our parishioners died on that fateful night.

parishofthegoodshepherd.uk/history-of-st-pauls-church

Photograph: Mary Huntley

EVERYWHERE MEANS SOMETHING TO SOMEONE

The thing is that Dover *is* this river, that's it. Dover itself isn't really what people say — I learned this from working with local people. When I ask, "Where do you live?" Ah, Elms Vale, Buckland, Tower Hamlets... nobody actually says they live in Dover. They're all tributaries of the river, so they're a bit like Welsh valleys.

I mean the houses either side are stepped up as if they were on the river course; you have the main river course which is the Dour, which has made the harbour and provided all the energy for all these industries along its banks. Then you have these tributaries that have been built up either side and everyone has a view — it's true, everyone has an amazing view.

There are deprived wards in Dover, and when you go up and explore them, they are right on the edge of the Kent Downs, and there's been a lot of thought put into the building of the developments as well. Everyone's got a garden, and everyone has got a view, so there is a lot of beauty too.

Photograph: Strange Cargo

EVERYWHERE MEANS SOMETHING TO SOMEONE

ST EDMUND'S CHAPEL

/// ACTIVE.WORRY.POCKET

The chapel was built in 1253 and is the smallest chapel still in use, with Sunday mass at 10am. It was built by the monks in the cemetery of St Martin's Priory for the poor. It was dedicated to St Edmund by St Richard de Wych, Bishop of Chichester, who died three days later. His entrails were buried in the chapel. The chapel was desecrated by Henry VIII, but it survived because it was used for other purposes. It disappeared from view and was forgotten for 400 years — it was even used as a smithy for a while.

It survived a second destruction when nearby buildings were bombed during the Second World War. You can see it fully from Priory Street; at one point it was completely surrounded by buildings, and was only revealed when they were demolished. They have vigils and cello performances in there, it's so atmospheric. It's just an extraordinary building, and probably my favourite building in Dover.

It escaped demolition in the 1960s when the council was eager to widen the road. There are cobbles on the stone floor and pilgrims would kneel on these as a penance. Some brought a pebble with a hole in when landing on Dover beach and place it outside the chapel. When the chapel was renovated, they were found.

stedmundschapel.co.uk

Photograph: Paul Smye-Rumsby

EVERYWHERE MEANS SOMETHING TO SOMEONE

I volunteer for this, helping people who have onset or signs of dementia, and their carers. They come along for a bit of respite. The major thing is loneliness for the elderly, it's prolific.

I had major surgery recently and went up to King's in London. Before I went up for surgery, I was in Ashford hospital and on my ward there were three women with dementia. One of them would say to me, "Come on, we've got to get the ship," and I was going, "Alright, I'll come along in a minute." Within a second she'd forget, and be doing something else. The staff were run ragged, and I was just managing the three dementia patients. The nurses said, "You should work with people with dementia, because you're a natural." I would play Scrabble with them, giving them time, and the staff just couldn't because they were firefighting.

Dover Smart do creative activities here: drawing, painting, printmaking, all sorts. They help lots of people in need of support. I've been helping for eight months. People come in for a chat and a cup of tea. It's a social place and it's community-building. It's a bit of a lifeline having this space.

Photograph: Rebecca Sperini

Shakespeare frequently visited Dover at the time of writing *King Lear*. I heard a radio show about Dover Cliffs quoted in *King Lear*, where the character Gloucester has had his eyes gouged out and he is flung out of the house and told to "smell his way to Dover," as he cannot see to find his way. There's this trickery by his friend who is disguised as a guide, so when Gloucester tries to commit suicide by throwing himself off the cliff, in reality he is still on flat ground and his guide pretends that God intervened to save his life, and that he had survived the fall. He pretends to look over the cliff and says, "Hangs one that gathers samphire, dreadful trade" — because people used to go down to collect samphire from the cliff face, to eat and sell, and very poor people would basically abseil off the edge of the cliff to harvest samphire. There's a duality to Dover cliffs, as they are gleaming white and gorgeous, but also sinister and mythic. When we watched *Jason and the Argonauts* and there's clashing cliffs that crush ships, they remind me of Dover. It became known as Shakespeare Cliff because of *King Lear*.

Photograph: Strange Cargo

EVERYWHERE MEANS SOMETHING TO SOMEONE

Dover feels as if it's a valve to the continent. What I've always loved about Dover is that it's a border town, its feels like a border town to me. It feels like this weird, thin place with these really complex layers of history. It's a place of passing and traffic. Of comings and goings. And the life here, the kind of day to day life is this weird mildness, and you spectate all of this passing and you feel as if you are under an underpass, and unnoticed, and that's kind of what I like about it. Then there's this surge of activity and it's all about the border and the barrier, and our private lives are simultaneously in the shadows, and in the sunlight — the way the cliffs reflect the light, it's like a giant photographer's reflector of refracted light.

Photograph: Strange Cargo

EVERYWHERE MEANS SOMETHING TO SOMEONE

In Dover, when there was no television, you went to the pictures. There used to be four cinemas in Dover. So you'd go to the pictures, and you'd come out at ten o'clock, and the pubs would be throwing out at ten o'clock. So, from ten o'clock onwards the town was crowded, people were going all over the place. There was a sense of community.

When I was a teenager... can you remember the film *Dracula*, the original? I was about fourteen when that came out. I went to the cinema by myself; I went to the Odeon that was on London Road. Anyway, I sat there scared out of my mind. I came out of the picture house and thought, I do not fancy going up the Castle where I lived in the dark by myself.

So I walked round all the pubs, looking for my mum and dad. I found them eventually. I shouldn't have been in the pub really, I walked in there and my dad said, "Oh, what are you doing here?" and I said, "I just fancied coming to find you." But the real reason was I was too scared to go back to the Castle alone.

Photograph: Susan Pilcher

So many happy memories — always beginning with which entrance to choose. The lower gate with the long climb first to the bird cage, and then to the playground... small children are likely to need dragging up! The middle, hidden gate which took you to the best climbing trees and where families had a picnic on 'the flat bit'. The side gate, which led you to the winding tree-lined adventure route which was cross country hell for me at secondary school. Finally, you could choose the top gate, just a stone's throw from the Castle, and with the best views across Dover town.

In the 80s my dad used to hold an event called the Dover Pageant at this park. On the main tennis courts were historical re-enactments, period dancing, Maypole, chariot racing. The top courts were a boot fair. A celebration of history in a historic town.

In terms of the best way to get home from the park, without doubt it's on a sledge down the steep banks, weaving between trees and trying to make sure you don't end up in the pond with the frogs and the goldfish.

Photograph: Susan Pilcher

My dad and I have an old car, and when we were rebuilding the engine we needed a length of a specific type of hose. His next door neighbour recommended we try Ardee Hose — a whole shop dedicated to hose! So we went down and asked them, and the man took us into the back of this incredible shop and workshop, which extended into a tunnel dug into the cliff behind. It got colder and colder the further we went into the shop. Of course, they had just the thing we wanted, and they cut it to length for us too. We left the shop impressed, both with their knowledge and stock, and their use of a tunnel for storing lengths of hose — it couldn't have been more suited to the job!

....

If you'd have come here last week there were baby robins everywhere, the wildlife seems to do well in here. I've been here for about 18 years, but I didn't start the business, it's been here far longer than that. The building goes right back into the cliff. Most of our stuff is for the ships; for marine customers. People come in for all sorts of things and if we can help them we will. We make up hydraulic pipework mostly, that's our main business. There was a foundry in here many years ago, but it caught fire. The foundry made all sorts of things cast in sand, like weightlifting discs and lots of other things.

Photograph: Strange Cargo

My father had one of these ancient sorts of jobs called a Turn Cock. Up in the Castle — it was the barracks in those days, with all the regiments — and he'd go around the whole area regulating the water supplies going through. Water was shunted all over the place. He used to have to walk around with this big, massive key and open up these stop cocks in roads and turn one off, turn another off, and he used to have to do this at night when no one was using the water.

We lived in the Castle for about 15 years. I was about ten when I went up there, in about 1950ish. We lived in a debtors' prison — 300 years ago, falling behind on payments could land you in this prison. It was later turned into housing, and still stands today. If you walk towards the Castle, up the road, you see the tower and it's got a sign on it: 'the Debtors' Prison', and that's where we lived. I didn't realise until I saw it in a book — I opened this book and saw my house and thought, I lived there!

Photograph: Alan Duncan Photography
(alanduncan.com)

When you sail into Dover you can see a balcony cut into the White Cliffs. As a child I found it so intriguing, but the tunnel remained closed and the route through to it a mystery. The Castle has many underground secrets open to explore, and they were always my favourite adventures. I remember the first time I climbed down the damp, dark, spiralling staircase to the dungeons. And when I found the secret passageway behind the ammunition magazines, I kept that secret close to my chest. The rooms under the lookout platform were a hideout just for me. The hidden chapel was a magical space that few knew existed, and finding the passageway between the staircases and looking through the slits in the wall to the people below; I felt like the master of spies. The Castle experience has a bit more staging nowadays, so you need less imagination in the ruined façades. But one of my most powerful memories was the first time I stood on that balcony, cut into the cliffs, when they finally opened up the tunnels. I imagined myself on a ferry heading out to France, watching in awe as a someone stood waving from the secret opening within the famous White Cliffs of Dover.

Photograph: Amy West

EVERYWHERE MEANS SOMETHING TO SOMEONE

In St Radigund's they refer to Tower Hamlets as 'them over the hill', as if they were goblins or something. It's a titchy, little place anyway, like a village. You never meet someone that says they live in Dover: they live in Elms Vale, Tower Hamlets, Buckland, St Radigund's… This is Castle where we are; River is its own little world. You go through that tunnel under the railway, and suddenly you're in middle class world. With Kearsney at the end, Crabble Mill and the rugby ground. You can see as you walk down there past houses, there's a music stand in the front room and you realise, ah, the kids are learning the violin.

....

Dover's association with cricket ended when Kent stopped playing at Crabble. A lot of people go dewy-eyed about that, as it was one of the Kent County cricket grounds. They used to have cricket weeks and the big stars at the time used to come to play.

Photograph: Strange Cargo

EVERYWHERE MEANS SOMETHING TO SOMEONE

Pencester Gardens was a great place to go after school. As 11-year-olds we'd play hide and seek there in the summer months with school friends, after we'd had dinner. Parents had to just hope we'd come back when we were told, as they had no way of contacting us.

Photograph: Strange Cargo

Enduring memories for me include the long walk from Clarendon Road down Folkestone Road to town, supermarket shopping in Lipton's, which later became Etam, but now stands empty.

Lipton's, which I recall was Dover's only supermarket, was the place to buy basics like Mother's Pride bread — meat and veg was bought daily from the butchers and greengrocers local to our house.

We paid for our rented TV at Rediffusion in Priory Court Road. We had to stand up and change the three channels on the telly by using a switch on the wall.

I remember living on Clarendon Road, playing out in the street and knocking on neighbours' doors asking if Jane was coming out to play. Running up and down shouting and being shouted at by an older generation to, "Clear off to your own end of the street!"

We loved it when the dustbin men came, and we knew them all by name.

Photograph: Rebecca Sperini

EVERYWHERE MEANS SOMETHING TO SOMEONE

Where I live up by Noah's Ark Road, near Dover Grammar School, as you walk down the road there's just a steel door and behind that is a tunnel that runs all the way down to Coombe Valley. I know once or twice it has been opened, but I don't know what condition it is in now. I don't know whether it's true, but only some of the Dover tunnels have been unearthed, and it's rumoured that there are tunnels that go all the way from the Castle right up to Western Heights. Up at the Castle they're still uncovering new tunnels.

Photograph: Rebecca Sperini

EVERYWHERE MEANS SOMETHING TO SOMEONE

Bradley: I walk all over Dover, because of Pokémon Go. I've caught some really good Pokémons in Connaught Park — it's a big area, so I've got a couple of rare ones there. I also got good ones at Market Square and also the seafront. You can't go there and get the same Pokémon because they respawn and randomise.

Emma-Dawn: The rarest Pokémon I've caught is a Salamence, which is a dragon. Do you know Londis, the shop at Dolphin House? I caught it there. It was THE most random place for THE most random Pokémon.

Bradley: I've never caught that one. I want to though. I'm looking out for it.

Emma-Dawn: I was never interested in the show, but I like the game because it gets me out walking around Dover.

Bradley: So now I make my own Pokémon cards with the different art types we learn at the youth club.

Photograph: Rebecca Sperini

This was Alan Hughes, a traditional tailors and menswear shop for about 40 years. People still tell us they bought their wedding suit or school uniform here; it was the sort of place where you could buy a cummerbund and bow tie. When we took it over it still had the original display window and shelving for various clothing. A long time before that it was a Chinese laundry, or food supplier, something with a Chinese connection.

We thought that Dover was missing that little niche wine bar, so we have lots of wines on the menu. We're a music venue, bringing different sorts of music, art exhibitions, talks, popular music and jazz. We aspire to be one of the only late-night jazz outlets outside of London. We try to have a mixed offer and something new to Dover. It's really welcoming. We have women who tell us they feel very comfortable coming here on their own too, which is great. There's always quality wine on the menu and we serve a cheese board and local meats. We deal with local vineyards which make great wines, particularly sparkling wines. Some of the big French champagne houses own land over here now.

Photograph: Rebecca Sperini

I've lived in Dover my entire life — even after 25 years. I've got a flat on the same street that I moved into in 1997. Dover truly is the only home I've ever known. I've worked in some amazing places, like the original Kearsney Abbey tea rooms, and even in the iconic Castle itself — but my most memorable moment has to be watching the recently renovated Market Square begin a new life following its renovations in 2021.

I began working at The Market Square Kitchen in October of 2021, a business that used to be the famous Dickens Bakery on Castle Street, which found fame in Charles Dickens's 1850 novel *David Copperfield*. This was just before the groundworks began on the Market Square and, after almost an entire year of constant construction, we were thrilled to be front-and-centre for the grand unveiling in August 2022. An artisan market was held to commemorate the event, and a renewed sense of life has returned. Following the success, there's a cautious optimism that's being felt now — and, as someone who has seen Dover change drastically over 25 years, it's nice to know there's still a beating heart at the centre of this town.

Photograph: Strange Cargo

Finish# OLD METROPOLE HOTEL, BIGGIN STREET

/// SHEETS.REACT.WEDGE.

This magnificent building used to be the old Metropole Hotel. You can still see the initials M H on the balconies. I have been inside, and the flats are beautiful, you can tell it's a quality building by the beautiful windows. Someone once asked me, where is there lift? There should be a lift inside. But what had happened was that Wetherspoon's, which occupies the whole of the street level of the building, built right up to the lift door and blocked it off, so the lift is still inside, but there is no way to get to it. As far as I know it's all still there.

Photograph: Rebecca Sperini

EVERYWHERE MEANS SOMETHING TO SOMEONE

I very, very rarely go out to eat, but if I do it would be Nando's or Kaspa's.

I like Kaspa's because it's a place I go on my birthday and where I meet my friend Serran from school. We order different things to each other, but I order banana waffle every time with ice cream. It's a birthday tradition now. Although once it was like the summertime, and I had Covid, and I was really upset about it. So even though it wasn't my birthday, my mum ordered me a Kaspa's to cheer me up. I didn't really eat it because I felt so unwell, and it was really sad.

It's better to go in there than order because it's like black and lots of pink lights, it's nice in there. There's music playing and other people my age.

Photograph: Susan Pilcher

I used to work as an employee for English Heritage at Dover Castle, and as I walked into work, this was my view from atop the battlements — looking down onto the town of Dover before a shift was certainly a great way to start the day!

Photograph: Jake Michael

My first school was an infant school called Belgrave on Belgrave Road. I went there from the age of five to seven. It was about half a mile from my house, and all the local children went there. We used to walk on our own as there were no roads to cross. We had free milk, and a rich tea biscuit was halfpenny. There was no school uniform. It was an excellent school, and I remember really enjoying it there, although once I was talking in assembly and got sent behind the piano for being naughty. I seem to remember one local boy always climbed up the lamp posts on the way home.

Photograph: Rebecca Sperini

I've lived in Dover since 1965. My dad was a headmaster and mum a teacher, working together at Sibertswold School in Shepherdswell. We moved to Marlborough Road when the top half had just been built. Contractors were still doing finishing touches — our address was known as 'Plot 97' for over a year, which is how long it took to be allocated house numbers by the Post Office. My sister Alison and I attended St Martin's Primary School. I had a crush on Phillipa Dean there, whose brother did artwork for some rock band... turns out my favourite band was and still is YES, and that the band's artist Roger Dean is famous in so many folks' eyes. The Dean family lived in the Elm Park Gardens area. We're still living in Elms Vale, where I play the music of (amongst other bands) YES in my radio shows on DCRfm 104.9fm. We've seen so many changes in Dover, including the loss of the railway line along the seafront. The best features, for us, are the St James's area and the Marina Curve. So, looking forward to the regeneration and council investment in Dover town.

Photograph: Rebecca Sperini

Wilfred 'Billie' Neville was a pupil at Dover College and a Captain with the East Surrey Regiment during the First World War. He took two footballs with him into the trenches and, on 1 July 1916, Wilfred's division was given orders to go over the top and capture German trenches 200 yards away. In a letter to Wilfred's sister, his colleague 2nd Lieutenant CW Alcock describes what happened next: "There were two footballs, and on one was printed 'The Great European Cup-Tie Final. East Surreys v Bavarians. Kick off at zero.' On the other in large letters was this: 'NO REFEREE', which was W's way of telling the men they needn't treat the enemy too gently. Five minutes before 'zero' hour your brother strolled up in his usual calm way and we shared a last joke before going over. The Company went over the top very well, with Soames and your brother kicking off with the Company footballs."

Together they dribbled and kicked the balls towards the Germans. Billie Neville was shot and killed right in front of the German trenches, but because of the 'Football Charge', his men accomplished their objective. Billie is always remembered for how brave and courageous he was the day he died, and for how charismatic and funny he was all the days that he lived. Following his death, a poem was published in *The Daily Mail:*

On through the hail of slaughter, where gallant comrades fall; Where blood is poured like water, they drive the trickling ball; The fear of death before them is but an empty name; True to the land that bore them, the SURREYS played the game.

There's a bronze statue by sculptor Hannah Stewart of Billie in Dover College grounds.

Photograph: Hannah Stewart

EVERYWHERE MEANS SOMETHING TO SOMEONE

EVERYWHERE MEANS SOMETHING TO SOMEONE

'ison Burton, Town Clerk at Dover Town Council for commissioning *The People's* 'or her support and patience throughout the project. Thanks too to the team 'ly Karen Dry and Tracey Hubbard; and to Aarron Monaco and Destination 'edge in reaching into the community. Your confidence in our work has . Thanks to Dover Town Council elected councillors who have been so

362, 374, 394, 426, 442, 444, 84, 22, 144, 186, 74, 526, 358, 26, 234, 40, 8,

,rateful to everyone who spread the word about the project to local people and g gather stories across the town, including the Dover Greeters team; Jon Iveson at um; Martin Crowther at Maison Dieu; Christopher Seadon at Dover Community Radio; ones at DAD; Lisa Oulton at Future Foundry; and Frazer Doyle at Dover Pride. And thank you .ne local social media groups who shared our invitation to contribute to the Guidebook.

strange Cargo would like to thank Peter Cocks for writing the foreword; our dedicated research team and location photographers for their brilliant work collecting facts, stories and anecdotes from participants and photographing the locations, including Brigitte Orasinski, Hannah Prizeman, Richie Moment, Amy West, Susan Pilcher, Rebecca Sperini, Mary Glow, and to all the photographers whose beautiful photographs of Dover grace this Guidebook. Each photographer is credited alongside their image.

And finally, to Scarlett Rickard for producing the graphic design for our marketing campaign and for assembling the print layout for this very substantial guidebook. www.scarlettrickard.co.uk

www.strangecargo.org.uk   @strangecargoart